BODYGUARDS
The World of VIP Protection

This book is dedicated to the men and women prepared to die taking a bullet meant to kill someone else. They call themselves simply, but aptly, bodyguards.

BODYGUARDS
The World of VIP Protection

RICHARD O'CONNOR

ARMS AND
ARMOUR

Arms and Armour Press
An Imprint of the Cassell Group
Wellington House, 125 Strand, London WC2R 0BB

Distributed in the USA by Sterling Publishing Co. Inc.,
387 Park Avenue South, New York, NY 10016-8810.

British Library Cataloguing-in-Publication Data:
a catalogue record for this book is available from the
British Library

ISBN 1-85409-322-3

Designed and edited by DAG Publications Ltd.
Designed by David Gibbons; edited by Philip Jarrett;
printed and bound in Great Britain.
Printed and bound in Great Britain by
Hartnolls Limited, Bodmin, Cornwall

Contents

Acknowledgements

Bodyguards: The World of VIP Protection was made possible only with the brave co-operation of the countless personal protection officers who spoke openly and honestly about their profession. Their dignity, courage and sense of humour guided me through their world, a world in which only the best will do, in which mistakes cost lives, and in which the price for failure is death. To attempt to thank them all by name would take a book in itself, and while many who helped were prepared to place their names on record, others preferred anonymity; a choice I fully understand. I wish to thank them all for showing confidence and trust, and hope the book truly reflects their profession.

Others whom I can mention, I hope, without breaking trust are my saviour, Roderick Dymott, who helped enormously from the beginning with suggestions on structure and content; his editorial team, who changed the incomprehensible jargon into readable prose; and most of all my girlfriend Kim, for her patience and forbearance with my secrecy and unscheduled disappearances.

6

Introduction

Close Protection has always been one of the most misunderstood occupations in the world. The public sees the dapper figure standing ominously behind a head of state as an unnecessary luxury, which, more often than not, they pay for. Bodyguarding is also associated with the excitement of a Hollywood movie and the globetrotting travel of a corporate executive from a multinational conglomerate. Yet in the real world the business is one of highs, lows, boredom and frustration, allied to monotonous routine.

In a society that has seen a threefold increase in the random killing of VIPs, committed by the envious, deprived or fearful, and in which the number of VIPs at risk, in Britain alone, now runs into six figures, the assassin has become the government's number one enemy. Gone are the days when armed guardians were only deployed in the time known as 'Transition to War'. Today, bodyguards can be found at every level of social stratum, protecting people ranging from the low-level business executive to the President of the United States of America.

This escalation came about not by accident or design, but because of the threat created by terrorism. Terrorism, and terrorism alone, changed the way VIPs looked at assassination. In Britain the threat of death from trained assassination squads changed the way in which Members of Parliament were protected, especially after the mutilated body of Paddy Wilson, a prominent Northern Ireland politician, was found in a deserted quarry in the depths of the Irish countryside.

In the USA the case for personal protection was even stronger, even if direct acts of terrorism were an overseas problem, at least until the World Trade Centre bombing in 1994. But the lax gun laws, ever-increasing murder statistics and the pointless assassination of John Lennon in 1980 had the combined effect of tripling the need for body-guards, especially if you were rich.

This work is an attempt to analyse the craft of those employed within the world of Close Protection. It was never intended to be a manual for aspiring bodyguards; nor is it an attempt to sway public opinion or attain sympathy for the difficult job bodyguards do. However, to understand such a complex and closed world it is necessary to delve into recent history to see how the bodyguard business evolved into its current form, and, though it is not intended to rival Tony Geraghty's *The Bullet Catchers*, this book contains concise historical information on personal protection through the ages.

The research produced several unexpected conclusions. The first and most surprising is that the government-employed bodyguard is but a small cog in a much larger machine. The image of the lone officer standing gallantly between life and death is an image of the past. Today the Personal Protection Officer is not only supported by intelligence-gathering agencies, but also by bomb disposal experts, specialist search teams, police mobile escort groups and counter-assault teams. In this machine all the cogs, large and small, must intermesh and work in total synchronisation. If any one cog is even slightly out of line, the information vital to successful protection will fail to be passed up, down or across the chain of command, and ultimately the bodyguard on the ground will become all but useless.

The second surprise is that bodyguards, particularly those with the honour of protecting a head of state or government, are only as effective as he, or she, is allowed to be by the principal. Guarding members of a Royal Family can be both frustrating and nerve-wracking. Yet royalty live in the public spotlight from birth, becoming accustomed to the bodyguard as easily as they do to the many equerries and aides who pamper to their every need. Just as they listen with forbearance to their aides, they will also do likewise to their protection officer, for ignoring the latter could have much more far-reaching consequences.

The bodyguard, typecast with cropped hair, moustache, trench coat, identification pin and plastic tube running from ear to shirt collar, is prepared and ready to 'step into the line of fire' at a moment's notice, doing so in the knowledge that the expensive ballistic armour concealed beneath a tailored suit will stop bullets from all but the most powerful guns. Taking such a step is not an easy decision, but one that becomes instinctive. For the bodyguard is employed firstly to stop the VIP from entering a situation where the bodyguard's secondary skill – the use of firearms – will be required, and secondly to protect 'by whatever means necessary' should an assassin appear without warning.

Certain information contained within these pages could be of help to a potential assassin, so the names of bodyguards operating within sensitive government positions have been withheld. Many may disagree with this decision, arguing that those who opt for a career in close protection do so knowing the risks involved. Although I and the bodyguards themselves would agree with this, I feel that the families of personal protection officers should not be exposed or pay the price for their loved ones' choice of career.

On the advice of experts within the profession, I have also deliberately changed or omitted certain information on tactics, statistics and undisclosed technology used by bodyguards the world over. To many readers these changes will not be apparent, but to those within the industry they will be as obvious as night follows day. Again I make no apology for this, and hope that the reader will agree that it is necessary for their safety.

Where gender is expressed I have used the pronoun 'he' to enhance the book's readability. No offence is intended to the female reader. The book begins by describing how the bodyguard phenomenon grew and pinpointing its faults, then moves on to the threats posed to governments and their responses to them. It details training within the Secret Service, and delves into the work of bodyguards protecting politicians, diplomats and royalty. The bottom line of a bodyguard's job is his willingness to stand in front of a bullet meant to kill someone else, and this book tries to explain why someone would want to do such a thing. It concludes with a look at the private protection industry and the area now emerging as the world's number one operating centre for bodyguards: Russia.

Throughout, I have detailed all sides of the story, from the assassin and the victim to the bodyguard, who can be found, appropriately, standing between the former two. The odour of fear that pervades our society and touches democratic life across the globe has called for an armed response of which the bodyguard forms a part. Whether Her Majesty the Queen is opening a hospice in a back street in Birmingham to help the elderly, or South African leader Nelson Mandela is promoting a new housing estate in the ghettos of Soweto, bodyguards will be found standing nearby. This book allows you to stand there, too.

Richard O'Connor

1
Assassination

In 1963 Lord Home became the new British Prime Minister, the Pope died at the Vatican aged 81, and the city of Skopje in what was then Yugoslavia was destroyed by an earthquake. It was also the year in which the use of assassination as a tool to foster political coercion was accentuated. The violent killing of figures of authority elected by the people, or born into power and influence, called for a better breed of bodyguard.

Assassination has been practised for centuries. Julius Caesar, King Henri IV and Abraham Lincoln were all slaughtered by assassins. Yet it was always considered a Third World phenomenon, inspired by barbaric tyranny and ancient tribal conflicts. The assassination of élite public figures in the West was often carried out by those motivated by personal grudges or the desire to become famous. The exception was the killing of Archduke Franz Ferdinand in 1914, which ignited the flames of the First World War, but not even this assassination could compete with the killing of the world's most beloved presidential leader, John F. Kennedy, which shocked the world to its foundations and brought a country to its knees. Never before had a single event done so much to alter the fate of mankind. Today, Western security agencies and military bodyguard training teams across the world, including the German Civil Police and the British Special Air Service, use the Kennedy assassination to show prospective bodyguards how *not* to protect a VIP.

Admittedly, world leaders and top VIPs cannot even now be protected from every potential threat. Even those reputed to have impenetrable defences are vulnerable, as the killing of Indian Prime Minister Rajiv Gandhi showed. His assassin, standing in a crowd of well-wishers with 30lb of high explosives strapped to her body, detonated the fuse as he stepped forward to shake her hand. The new threat of the fanatical suicide bomber had arrived. But can the killing of a president or prime minister change the fabric of modern society? Sadly, it can.

The importance of the Kennedy assassination to modern thinking, so far as personal protection is concerned, is illustrated in a recent US survey, which showed that although nine out of ten adult Americans were unable to name the killer of another US President, Abraham Lincoln, the same number easily named Kennedy's supposed assassin. On Friday 22 November 1963 President John F. Kennedy and his entourage flew to Love Field in Dallas to begin a 45-minute motorcade procession through the city leading to a luncheon speech at the Trade Mart building, but the President died in a hail of bullets in the ultimate *coup d'état* that launched the Vietnam war. Responsibility for the protection of the President that day lay solely in the hands of the Secret Service, a government organisation tasked with protecting the President, whether he liked it or not, since the assassination of Lincoln in 1864. They were reputed to be the best bodyguards in the world, able to provide an impenetrable protective screen, but the reality was somewhat different. Presidential protection was riddled with gaping holes and unparalleled incompetence.

Historical figures of authority had always scorned their imposed guardians, often refusing to be restricted in their daily movements and playing down their bodyguards' concerns as superstitious nonsense. President Kennedy was no exception, but the belief that legitimate governments did not need excessive protection was changed that momentous day in Dallas in 1963. On 27 November the Secret Service carried out a reconstruction of the assassination and identified many areas of fault that were instrumental in the assassination's success and, if rectified beforehand, could have prevented the killing. A particular item was the advance media coverage of the proposed visit. The trip to Dallas was announced after White House officials had approved the route on 18 November. Details of the motorcade's route, including maps and timings, began to appear in local newspapers the following day, and the Secret Service chief, James Rowley, quickly realised that the advance publicity had given the assassins vital information to enable them to execute their plan. In response, future announcements on presidential visits were issued on a 'need to know' basis, with no advance warning being given and only selected journalists being informed. It was a lesson which would not be learnt by British body-guards until the attempted assassination of Prime Minister Margaret Thatcher in 1984.

The Kennedy assassination marked a turning point in bodyguard procedures, which were orientated towards lone deranged assassins using low-calibre pistols, which history had shown to be the most common scenario. Before 1963 the use of sniper fire to assassinate prominent figures was only available to a few highly trained ex-mili-tary personal, and was rarely, if ever, used. But the Kennedy assassi-nation heralded the dawning of the 'stand-off' assassin, able to use sophisticated weaponry and advanced tactics to their fullest effect. To reduce the risk from successful sniper fire in the future, the Secret Ser-vice increased its manpower threefold to provide a thicker screen of human shields, and this was easily visible at the President's state funeral three days later.

Western government protection agencies of the time, including the Secret Service, believed that deterrence was the best form of defence. Yet when that deterrence failed, the bodyguards were unprepared to deliver what they claimed to provide – protection. This was a fact that bodyguards employed by African states would not learn for another decade. On that fateful day the White House detail certainly looked the part, but when the shooting started they were no more than spectators to their own failings. One improvement made after the killing was the recommendation that the President's physician should accompany him on all of his travels and occupy 'a position near to his side'. This was ini-tially considered unfeasible by the Secret Service, but a compromise was reached to the effect that all White House bodyguards should be trained to an advanced paramedic standard. The President's doctor was even-tually accommodated in a specially designed ambulance concealed in one of the back-up vehicles, but only after the attempt on Ronald Rea-gan's life in March 1981, when he was hit in the shoulder by a ricochet from shots fired at him by John Hinkley. The 'ambulance' that is now used not only contains the President's blood type, but other advanced surgical equipment to deal with bomb blast and gunshot wounds; an idea now adopted by many European leaders.

Much criticism was directed towards the Secret Service after the assassination, mainly aimed at the preventive capabilities the agency had in place. One fault was that the Service could only deal with 'direct threats against the President' and, in particular, with 'individuals who had threatened to kill him'. The agency's Protective Research Section was responsible for collating and disseminating this information but, because of a lack of trained personnel and proficient technical assistance, the Service largely relied upon other Federal or State agencies, including the Federal Bureau of Investigation (FBI) and Central Intelligence Agency (CIA). But while the FBI had secured extensive information on the alleged assassin, Lee Harvey Oswald, it had no official requirement to pass this on to the Secret Service. The lack of co-ordination between these agencies led to a breakdown in communication and a failure to provide adequate protection. The Warren Commission, set up to investigate the assassination, concluded that 'the FBI and Secret Service took a restricted view of their roles in preventive intelligence work prior to the assassination'.

Today, Federal agencies are connected via secure satellite communication with other intelligence agencies worldwide, allowing an instant exchange of information on potential assassins and threats. The Kennedy killing heralded the beginning of the bodyguard boom which swept America over the next five years. Both government and private agencies increased the resources and manpower to cope with the growing paranoia of top politicians and elder statesmen. The rich and élitist area of Hollywood turned into a city under siege as egotistical film stars became obsessed with assassination and hired masses of personal bodyguards, justifying their actions by saying: 'If they can kill a president, they can kill little old me'.

However, those first years were dogged by incompetent and unprofessional protection as many companies continued to rely on aggressive visible deterrence rather than the passive ability to react effectively if an assassin struck, something the Secret Service had learnt to its cost and long since improved. The assassination of civil rights leader and Black Muslim minister Malcolm X in February 1966 illustrated this point. He was shot dead by three assailants as he prepared to make a speech at the Audubon Ballroom in New York, after his bodyguards had left his side to eject an argumentative member of the audience who had set off a smoke bomb. These faults were slowly rectified as many ex-Secret Service agents moved into the private protection industry after leaving the White House detail owing to excessive working hours and their increasing age. Government protection was fast becoming a young man's job, with overtime in excess of 30 hours a week and the stress to match. Some VIPs preferred to leave their protection in the hands of the Almighty. Two such people were Dr Martin Luther King and Robert Kennedy, both assassinated in 1968, proving that those who chose the Deity for protection normally ended up dead.

Dr King, the pre-eminent black civil rights worker and Nobel Prize Winner, was shot in the face as he stepped out on to the second-floor balcony of the Lorraine Motel overlooking Memphis's black ghetto. Dr King received over 40 death threats a day from members of the Klu Klux Klan and Nazi Party, and though he did use bodyguards for a time after he was stabbed in New York, he had fatefully turned them away three weeks before his own death. James Earl Ray was arrested for the assassination two months later at London Heathrow Airport, after eluding the FBI's manhunt in Canada and much of Europe. He was extradited to America, and after a short trial was sentenced to 99 years in prison.

It was Robert Kennedy who arranged for King's body to be flown back to his Atlanta home, but only two months later he too was the target of assassination, leaving the ill-fated Kennedy family mourning yet another death. Shortly after midnight on the night of 4 June, as Senator Kennedy was being led from the Ambassador Hotel in Los Angeles following a party connected with his seeking of the Democratic Party's Presidential nomination, shots rang out. Kennedy fell to the floor mortally wounded, and died some time later; five bystanders were also hit. Sirhan Bishara Sirhan, a Palestinian immigrant, was arrested and pleaded guilty to the crime. His death sentence was later commuted to life imprisonment after the State abolished the death penalty.

Although Senator Kennedy was assured of the presidential nomination and favoured to be the nation's next leader, he was offered no bodyguard protection and refused to employ any. The hotel did take steps to improve security that night by hiring extra security guards from the Ace Guard Service to act as bodyguards, one of whom, Thane Eugene Cesar, walked directly behind and to Kennedy's right as they left the hotel. Eyewitnesses to the assassination, including those hit by stray bullets, fixed the closest distance between Sirhan's gun and Kennedy as no less than one yard to his front, yet the autopsy report concluded that Kennedy had died from 'a fatal gunshot wound to the head fired from within one inch of Kennedy's right ear', and that all shots hit Kennedy 'from behind, sharply below and to the right'. Ballistics tests also proved that the fatal bullet 'had not come from Sirhan's gun'. Cesar admitted that when Sirhan began firing he removed his revolver and 'returned fire', but denied hitting Kennedy as he did so. However, FBI investigators found no rounds missing from the revolver when they examined it some hours later, and forensic tests proved the gun had not been fired. It then emerged that Cesar had a second gun, but the weapon disappeared before experts could examine it. If Cesar was the true assassin, then his use of the confusion and mayhem of the moment to kill Senator Kennedy was both resourceful and shrewd. It would also make the Senator's killing one of the first assassinations in modern history to be committed by a person employed to protect.

In the same year as Robert Kennedy's killing, the Western world became the target for terrorism, albeit on a small scale, as the Popular Front for the Liberation of Palestine moved its fight from the Occupied Territories into Europe. Palestinian terrorists had waged irregular warfare against the Israelis for some years, but the total news blackout and rigid censorship inside the country reduced their potential audience and led to a failure to undermine the government, even though their military operations were a great success. Palestinian terrorists needed to capture the world's attention to keep their fight alive, and Europe offered this 'first generation' of terrorists numerous unprotected embassies and commissions, plus mass-media coverage. The Palestinians chose their targets carefully, and predominantly from those countries which openly supported Israel. The established governments of America, Britain, Germany and France became the targets for this new deadly war of terrorism, and none of them had the facilities or the expertise to counter the threats from skyjacking, assassination, abduction and bomb attacks. The Palestinian terrorists created the foundation for the building and development of other terror organisations, and there have been no boundaries to the global coverage of terrorist formations, with more than 125 organisations in 50 countries.

Bonn and Paris took the threats of assassination and acts of air piracy very seriously, increasing top VIP protection fourfold and updating security of key buildings around the globe. Yet Whitehall remained unconcerned and refused to agree to additional funds for ministerial protection, even though London saw an increase in terrorist incidents after the hit-and-run machine-gun attack on the American Embassy in 1967 and the birth of 'Irish terrorism' in Northern Ireland two years later. Though the government was slow to react to the growing threat and stood fast on increasing its own protection, it did instruct the military élite of the Special Air Service (SAS) to send a handful of soldiers to protect selected overseas VIPs who were considered too important to lose. The SAS had already anticipated this with the formation in 1967 of the Bodyguard Training and Advisory Team, supplemented four years later by the expansion of the Counter Revolutionary Warfare Wing (see Chapter 2). The SAS was now able to call on its experience of conflicts in many regions of the world to enhance its protection expertise, yet was unable to hone its skills on the streets of Britain owing to the political fear that it would be misconceived by the media. Ministerial protection therefore remained in the firm hands of Scotland Yard, but with the help and training of the SAS behind closed doors in Hereford.

In addition, the SAS protection teams were requested to provide bodyguard training to many African states when the Third World was thrown into turmoil after a spate of coups, counter-coups and assassinations. This was achieved through a conduit of private security com-

17

panies run by ex-SAS officers, including Kini Mini Services (once an informal codeword among SAS soldiers meaning 'deniable operations'), Control Risks, WinGuard and WatchGuard, to lessen the embarrassment to the government if things went wrong. The killings started in 1969 with Kenyan government minister and potential future national leader Tom Mboya, who was shot dead as he left a shop in Nairobi accompanied by his bodyguard, who did little except stand and weep. His murder deprived Africa of a gifted moderate capable of bringing peace to the many warring factions, and served only to plunge Kenya back into a spate of tribal killings.

Sixty per cent of African states were affected by the many coups and assassinations before the SAS arrived. Included in this statistic were Dr Ali Shermarke, the President of Somalia, assassinated during a military coup, and Sheikh Abeid Karume, the dictator of the Peoples' Republic of Zanzibar, killed by Lieutenant Hamud, who riddled the tyrant with machine-gun fire as he played cards with his bodyguards, who returned fire and killed the assassin.

The standard of African bodyguards improved drastically after the military training teams arrived, and this is reflected in the fact that there were no political assassinations from 1978 to 1994. This fragile peace was shattered in April 1994, when the Rwandan presidential aeroplane was hit by two surface-to-air missiles as it came in to land at Kagali airport, killing Juvenal Habyanmana, the country's President, and Cyprien Ntaryarmira, President of Burundi. The horror of civil war in Africa erupted once again.

European terrorism still posed the greatest threat to Western bodyguards, but like their counterparts in America a decade earlier, they were only trained to cope with the lone schizophrenic killer. When the well-equipped and determined terrorists began their excursions of death across the continent they were caught totally off guard. Security services were under-resourced and overstretched to provide protection to the increasing number of potential targets. Bodyguards found themselves increasingly outnumbered as terrorism expanded, and its practitioners did not adhere to the rules of the Geneva Convention. Protection teams could only watch helplessly as terrorism claimed victim after victim. Spanish Prime Minister Carrero Blanco was one of the first to fall victim, killed by the separatist movement Euskadi ta Askatasuna (ETA) in 1973. They had at first planned to kidnap Blanco, but after he was appointed Head of Government and his security was upgraded, the plan was changed to assassination. On 20 December, as Blanco returned to his office from morning mass in his official armour-plated limousine, an explosion catapulted the vehicle 40ft into the air, causing it to hit a church parapet. The bomb, which had been concealed in a specially dug tunnel under the road, killed the Prime Minister, his chauffeur and bodyguards instantly. The assassination proved counter-productive for the Basque movement, serving only to bring Spain a step closer to democracy. However, it did show the extraordinary lengths to which terrorist organisations were prepared to go in an attempt to remove their target from the seat of power.

When assassination failed to destabilise governments, terrorists turned to abduction. The most notable case occurred in March 1978, when Aldo Moro, the former Prime Minister of Italy, was kidnapped and held hostage by Red Brigade terrorists. They demanded the release of thirteen fellow anarchists from Italian jails, but the government refused even to negotiate and Moro's body was found in a car boot some weeks later. He had been brutally slaughtered. Even though Moro was a former Prime Minister and tipped to be the next, he was afforded no protection.

Hans-Martin Schleyer, a West German industrial figurehead, was known to be a potential assassination victim and was provided with a team of police bodyguards, but he too was kidnapped and shot dead after 43 days in captivity. The case highlighted the terrorists' use of human compassion to achieve their goal, with the use of a woman pushing a pram to block the route and force the car to stop. The police driver was unwilling to take evasive action because of the risk of hitting the pram and killing the child, and he paid for the mistake with his life. British bodyguards detailed with some of the most sensitive protection duties in the world have admitted to the author that, faced with the same situation, they would have no hesitation in driving over a woman and baby to protect their client.

In a drastic effort to rebalance the scales, Western democracies banded together to counter this internationally financed form of conflict, supplied with weapons from Eastern Europe. In response to the killing of eleven Israeli athletes at the Munich Olympic Games in 1972, Germany formed its own anti-terrorist unit, Grenzschutzgruppe 9 (GSG9), and quickly took control of governmental protection until the German civil police were trained to a sufficiently proficient standard to be able to resume the responsibility. The unit's first commander, Ulrich Wegener, was an expert on terrorism, and soon formed lasting partnerships with many other special forces. These relationships were cultivated during years of cross-training and 'joint borrowing' of experienced soldiers for delicate operations, such as the one at Mogadishu airport in 1977, when two SAS soldiers aided GSG9 in rescuing 91 hostages from the hands of Palestinian terrorists. In return, GSG9 officers helped plan the Iran Embassy siege rescue at Prince's Gate in 1980. The German unit also introduced the powerful yet lightweight Heckler & Koch sub-machine pistols to Western bodyguards, and close-protection teams immediately added the MP5(K) short-barrelled pistol to their vast armouries.

The aim of terrorist organisations has always been to undermine and discredit Western governments, so naturally the aim of the political assassin forms a part of that overall strategy. However, this underlying objective was shattered in 1981, when it is thought terrorists played an important part in the first attempted assassination of the Pontiff. On 13 May, as the Pope made one of his famous and regular public appearances in St Peter's Square, Rome, Mehmet Ali Agca, a known and wanted convicted murderer, fired several shots over the heads of the gathered crowd, hitting the Pope, who slumped sideways, grimacing. The joyous occasion immediately turned to panic and confusion as people screamed and aides rushed to his side. Bystanders apprehended Agca and plain-clothed policemen in the crowd handcuffed him and spirited him away. Bodyguards who had mingled in the crowd moved forward to clear a route for the jeep, which raced off with other protection officers desperately administering first aid, including connecting the Pope to a plasma drip and injecting powerful painkillers. Two tourists who had also been wounded were carried to waiting ambulances.

The Pope, an energetic, dynamic, assertive and well-travelled leader of the Roman Catholic Church, had always enjoyed these Wednesday afternoon appearances, and said he drew strength from the gathered people. Both journalists and clergymen had expressed much concern over the small degree of protection the Pope requested, especially in such a violent age. Nevertheless he was a hard man to persuade of the importance of protection, and his regular appearances had continued unchanged.

An indication of the growing international co-operation between worldwide intelligence agencies after the Kennedy assassination became apparent soon after this incident, when it emerged that two weeks before the shooting the French intelligence organisation (SDECE) had sent two representatives to Rome to warn of an impending attack. Although he had listened, the Pope had done little to improve his security, though without his knowledge extra bodyguards were placed in the crowd that day. However, they could do little when the Pope was surrounded by such a mass of people. The reactions of those bodyguards close to the Pope immediately after the shooting are beyond reproach, and the medical attention he received on the way to hospital was impeccable, and arguably saved his life.

The assassin, Mehmet Ali Agca, aged 23, was an intelligent and determined terrorist. Having passed the entrance exam for a degree in economics at Istanbul University, he attended no classes. In February 1979 he carried out his first public killing, his victim being Abdi Ipekci, editor-in-chief of the nation's *Milliyet* newspaper. He was arrested and confessed to the killing in June of that year, but escaped from a maximum security prison five months later with the help of prison guards. In November, just before the Pope's visit to Turkey, Agca threatened to kill him in a letter to the *Milliyet*. The government took the prudent step of tightening already elaborate security, and the trip passed without incident. The following month Agca was actively involved in the killings of Ramazan Gunduz and Haydar Seyrangah, in revenge for their tipping-off of the police. It is believed that Agca carried out further terrorist training in Iran, Russia and Bulgaria before travelling to Rome, and it is said that he was offered DM 3 million to kill the Pope. After his arrest he refused to incriminate others and was sentenced to life imprisonment.

Agca opened the door to more attempts on the Pope; the first occurred as he convalesced, when a Spanish priest lunged at him with a bayonet. In 1985, during his visit to the Netherlands, a Turk named Samet Aslan was arrested for firearms charges and threatening the life of the Pontiff, and committed suicide in prison in 1987. A further attempt a year later resulted in the assassin's death after he had thrown a suspected parcel bomb over the gates of the Pope's summer palace. It was later found to contain rubbish.

Today the Pope makes few public appearances, mainly due to his age, failing health and the increasing threat of assassination. On the rare occasions he conducts open-air masses, security is heavy and crowds are kept at a considerable distance; a sad inheritance which the assassin's bullet has brought to the civilised world.

The 1979 elections in Britain brought to power a new Prime Minister, Margaret Thatcher, who had experienced at first hand the murders of politician Airey Neave and Earl Mountbatten some months before by the Provisional IRA. Upon her arrival in Downing Street she purchased two armoured Daimlers, tightened security around government buildings and increased protection for members of her cabinet. It was a far cry from the days when ministers could expect only a three-man protection team. Under Mrs Thatcher it tripled and, after the attempt on her life at the Tory party conference in 1984, the strength of Special Branch protection was expanded to over 1,200.

The SAS had been warning the government about chinks in its political protection for many years, but successive prime ministers had continually offered the same answer: 'democracy must be seen as an open system'. Although Mrs Thatcher did little to alter the statement, she would have added that it 'should be looked at through armour-plated glass'. The expansion in 1980 of the panel of Home Office experts regularly reviewing the threat posed to individual VIPs, to include the SAS Director of Operations and the Deputy Assistant

Commissioner of Special Branch Protection, was another sure sign that the new government took protection seriously.

The ensuing bodyguard boom was not on the scale of that in America, but politicians did change their social habits of a lifetime to combat the threat from IRA assassination squads stalking their constituencies. The British government, meanwhile, knew the IRA needed to score a 'big hit' to increase depleting funds from sympathisers. Threats to Mrs Thatcher had grown since the IRA hunger strikes in 1981, and so did her personal security. However, intelligence through informers had indicated that the most plausible assassination attempt would come from a surface-to-air missile attack on the helicopter she often used for local visits. Military intelligence had known for some time that it was 'highly probable' that the IRA possessed surface-to-air missiles, especially after the interception of arms shipments from Libya. But when the attack did come, at the Tory party conference in Brighton in 1984, it came from a totally unexpected quarter.

In the early hours of the morning, as the Prime Minister put the finishing touches to a speech she was to give later that day, a bomb concealed behind a wall panel in the bathroom of room 629 exploded, destroying the front of the hotel, killing four and injuring countless others. Amazingly, Mrs Thatcher walked away untouched but not unaffected. The bomber, Patrick Magee, was arrested eight months later during a police raid in Glasgow, and sentenced to life imprisonment. Three accomplices were also arrested, and provided anti-terrorist detectives with vital information that led to the recovery of 139lb of high explosive, extensive bomb-making equipment and plans to kill the SAS veteran General Sir Peter de la Billiere, who went on to command the British forces during the Gulf War.

The precision of the Brighton bomb, planted four floors above Mrs Thatcher's room, emphasised the expert training the IRA bombmakers had received from Middle Eastern terrorist organisations. It also marked the beginning of the use of 'sleeper' bombs to kill intended victims long after the terrorists had fled. Special Branch bodyguards, with the help of local police officers, had checked the hotel some days before the conference began, but failed to pick up the explosives odour with their sensitive detectors and sniffer dogs. In response to this new threat better detection equipment was purchased from American government agencies, one of which could detect the minute amounts of power emitted by a bomb's battery. The use and nature of other equipment retained by bodyguards in America, Australia and Britain is still classified, though recent articles in leading newspapers in Britain, identifying some of the new 'X-ray' equipment, has caused bewilderment within the security industry.

Today's Prime Minister is less reliant on bodyguard protection than his predecessor. However, the mortar bomb attack on Downing Street in 1991 served as a timely reminder that the assassins are still waiting for their opportunity to 'be lucky once'.

Although the main player in British terrorism, the IRA, declared a ceasefire, the short-lived peace process in Northern Ireland was unlikely to deter the global terrorist renegades or opportunist assassins from taking pot-shots at VIP targets. There will always be new activists waiting impatiently in the wings to take the stage of terror.

While Europe caught up with America in the standard of protection for high-risk VIPs, the Middle East remained impassive, and not even the premature death of Wasfi al-Tal, the Jordanian Prime Minister, shot dead as he left the Sheraton Hotel in Cairo, could induce a need for increased protection. Granted there were a few exceptions who employed high-profile bodyguards to keep assassins at bay, and some were even afforded the elaborate protection of SAS bodyguards for short, sensitive periods throughout the 1980s, like Sultan Qaboos shortly after he led the bloodless coup to end the oppressive reign of his father, Sultan Sa'id bin Taimur. Yet overall the standard was well below that in the rest of the world, and many prominent political figures were killed because of nothing more than ignorance.

The killing of President Anwar Sadat of Egypt in 1981, as he took the salute at a military parade, was an indication of the poor standard of bodyguard and a bitter blow for those seeking peace in the region. Sadat had signed a peace treaty with Israel, but was seen as a traitor to the Arab cause, and in particular to the Palestinian fight for self-rule. Although Sadat had an entourage of bodyguards that day, none was within arm's reach at the vital moment of his slaying, when rebel soldiers opened fire from the military parade organised in his honour. Yet the arrests that followed the killing pointed to a much deeper conspiracy than at first thought.

Two key players in the assassination later re-emerged during the World Trade Centre bombing in New York City in 1993. Sheikh Omar Abdul Rahman, a radical blind cleric and long-time opponent of the Mubarak government who had stood trial for conspiring to kill Sadat but had been acquitted owing to lack of evidence, was arrested and convicted of planning the Trade Centre bombing. The other was Emad Salem, an FBI informer who had arrived in the USA from Egypt three years before the bombing and offered his services as an informer. On the surface it appeared that Salem was just another Egyptian on the make, but it was later revealed that Salem was not only an Egyptian army officer, but one of Sadat's personal bodyguards present on the podium during the assassination. He had also been shot three times in the service of Egypt and honoured for his gallantry. Salem successfully infiltrated Rahman's inner circle by acting as the cleric's personal protection officer. However, after the group was arrested and convicted on Salem's evidence he disappeared, reportedly back to Egypt, though the Egyptian authorities refuse to admit or deny this.

The attempted assassination of political leaders, successful or otherwise, has always been a common feature of Middle Eastern life, with the PLO being both the victim and perpetrator. The killing of Arab expatriate cartoonist Ali-Adhami in 1987 was reputed to have been carried out by Abdul Rahmin Mustapha, one of Yasser Arafat's personal bodyguard, Force 17. The victims on the other side have included the PLO's London representative, Said Hammami, shot dead in his office. Hammami was thought to be negotiating with the Israelis to end the conflict in the Middle East on Arafat's behalf. At that time the PLO leadership was in a no-win situation, facing death if they made peace and death if they did not.

The Middle East was a dangerous area of operations for many bodyguards, with civil and urban conflicts in Beirut, the Gaza Strip and Palestine calling for an increase in Western bodyguards prepared to learn their trade the hard way. Yet personal protection officers working in the region were more concerned about kidnapping than assassination, as the abduction of Terry Waite by Islamic Jihad terrorists proved. His abduction also showed that bodyguards can only protect if allowed to do so by their client, and that those who refuse the advice of the protection team unwittingly promote their own demise. Terry Waite had dismissed his protection team as a show of trust toward the terrorists with whom he was negotiating for the release of other Western hostages. One bodyguard present at the time told the author: 'Against our best judgement and advice, Terry Waite decided to go it alone ... We could do nothing but sit and wait for the 'phone call we knew would come.'

Even up to 1986 there were still national leaders who spurned protective cover and thus hastened their own death. For example, Sweden had seen little political assassination activity in its history, but that changed on the last day of February 1986, when the country was rocked by the most astonishing killing since the murder of King Gustavus in 1792. Olaf Palme, the country's Prime Minister, was shot dead at point-blank range by a lone gunman using a Smith & Wesson revolver as he crossed a street in Stockholm with his wife. It transpired that Palme had dismissed his bodyguards, even though Swedish Intelligence had warned him that his life was in danger. He took the threat seriously but fatalistically. The murderer said nothing, and though there were witnesses no one could remember the killer's face, not even Lisbeth Palme. The assassin really was a shadow from the night. Unusually, no one claimed responsibility for the crime, and even though suspects were arrested and a large reward offered, the murderer remains unidentified. As public criticism mounted, resignations from government and police departments increased and rumours began of bribery and corruption, including payments to Indian politicians after a large military contract was awarded to Sweden by Indian Prime Minister Rajiv Gandhi. Nothing was proved, but the assassination of Gandhi some years later did little to lessen the suspicions.

One dictator has gone to extraordinary lengths in an attempt to obtain perfect protection, and understandably so. Saddam Hussein is a tyrant hated by his people and despised by the West. To counter the threat of premature death he has a military division, the 'Lions of Saddam', dedicated to his personal protection. He rarely leaves the confines of his palace bunker, and 'public appearances' are often performed by lookalike decoys or under controlled conditions. During the Gulf War Saddam was the target of many assassination attempts which his bodyguards successfully intercepted, and although the popular press have suggested that these were instigated by British and American special forces, this is unquestionably untrue. Killing Saddam Hussein would have proved counter-productive for the West, both politically and militarily, and would only have led to the collapse of Arab support for the coalition that eventually defeated the Iraqi army and gave the Americans a small but vital foothold in an oil-rich region of the world. Keeping Saddam alive also gave private security companies the opportunity to exploit the phobia that developed after the conflict, as many prominent businessmen feared the possibility of being abducted and used as 'human shields' by Iraq to minimise imposed sanctions.

The bodyguard boom finally reached the one area that truly needed it, and the following years saw an expansion of personal protection in the Middle East only previously surpassed in America. The Middle East still remains one of the most volatile areas, prone to regicide, tyrannicide and parricide. Nevertheless, political assassination of Western leaders is still not beyond the capabilities of many of the world's terrorist organisations, and though many terrorist organisations have recently been dissolved or sought peace, mainly owing to loss of support after the collapse of the Soviet Union, America has recently been the target of a growing number of internal terrorist bomb attacks on Federal buildings. The emphasis could so easily and quickly shift to assassination.

History shows that there are two types of assassin: the lone crank and the determined terrorist. The lone crank has often been rejected by society, craves the limelight and wishes to put the world to rights in one violent and sudden deed. These spontaneous killers are often inspired by media reports of other successful assassinations, a problem that has grown in Europe as news coverage by satellite and cable companies has mushroomed. The Secret Service admitted that, after the two failed assassination attempts on President Ford were shown live on American television, they were inundated with threats to finish the job which led to a Congressional review of presidential protection, though no improvements were recommended.

The assassination of John Lennon in December 1980 showed the world just how the lone crank assassin can shatter a modern society and dispose of such gifted people with no sign of remorse or repentance. For the bodyguard, lone cranks are the hardest threat to anticipate or intercept, as many decide to kill a public figure on impulse and conduct little or no prior surveillance. On the other hand, the political or contract killer rarely makes spontaneous decisions and, as a professional, he will avoid unnecessary exposure but will watch the intended victim for some time, often several months, to identify patterns and repetitions in routine or route. Bodyguards agree that counter-surveillance measures should pick up this activity, but add that they still do not have all the answers. Bearing in mind the fact that assassination has grown from the single use of a pistol at close range to the expertly hidden Semtex sleeper bomb concealed months in advance, one can understand their point of view.

Although the USA has been the country most affected by assassination, as highlighted in Dallas on that Fateful Friday in November 1963, it has developed into a world-wide tool of political subversion. Western leaders, by their very occupation, are prone to assassination and have come to accept death as an occupational hazard, whereas Third World heads of state appear to have death from the assassin's bullet written into their constitution and are prepared to stay in power only until the messengers of death decide to deliver the ultimate election vote, the *coup d'état*.

Personal protection has evolved into a profession that, in certain countries, has become more powerful than the VIPs it protects. The range of knowledge needed by bodyguards to combat the changing threat of assassination and keep themselves and their clients alive is formidable, and today protection officers insist that their clients wear bulletproof vests, work on the 'need to know' principle, use armoured limousines flanked by scores of motorcycle outriders and only travel on routes cleared in advance by specialised police units.

President Kennedy would never have accepted the measures that are used today to protect the world's prominent VIPs. But in contrast to the 1960s, ministers now realise that the threat from international terrorism far outweighs the public's appetite for political accessibility, and insist on having their homes patrolled and floodlit at night and equipped with a multitude of electronic gadgets to detect intruders, and have an entourage of bodyguards rarely out of arm's reach. They accept that foreign holidays are impossible, and are prepared to live like recluses, unable to visit friends or relatives even for the shortest time. The cost of such protection is no longer a burden for the governments concerned. Society has grown to accept the need to keep its VIPs alive, as it understands that the consequences of failure could be catastrophic for all.

Today's bodyguards admit they are fighting a macabre game of bomb and bullet, in which peace in Europe and the diminishing fear of Armageddon has led to an increase in irregular warfare, fought on the street of Europe and America by terrorists dedicated to proving that democracy is corrupt and that they, the combatants, will outlive the peacemakers. Being a bodyguard in modern society is not just about politely holding the car door open for the Prime Minister or flanking the President of the USA on state visits. It is about being, for a brief moment, the only defence left to society when the assassin strikes.

2
Meeting the Threat

Terrorism in Northern Ireland has been the bane of successive British governments for over 25 years. Close protection teams dispatched to the province to guard top army commanders and members of the judiciary came predominantly from military units such as the SAS and the Royal Military Police. Initially, their use caused widespread criticism within the corridors of power, but when Irish terrorism moved from sectarian murder toward political assassination, the government's decision was seen to be justified.

Three centuries of Irish history are laden with national dissatisfaction and local insurrection, as Protestants have fought Catholics over land, religion and politics. The British, often perched precariously between the two warring factions and smeared with pariah status, have tried in vain to relieve the tension by implementing new policies or injecting unlimited resources. One such policy, known as the Anglo-Irish Treaty, led to the creation of the Republic of Ireland in 1931 but failed to quell the rising tension, and only succeeded in deepening the already bitter hatred within the northern counties. The Belfast wing of the Irish Republican Army (IRA) resented the treaty in its entirety, and accused senior Dublin officials of 'selling out to the British'. It refused to toe the party line of acceptance, and the feud that erupted within its ranks soon after was inevitable, taking into account the fact that the north had more to lose from the treaty than it had to gain. But the defiant hard-liners in Belfast were to stand alone as the party voted in favour of the treaty, and the 'free state' came into being soon after. With the Catholic populace duly satisfied, the Belfast wing, which by now had renamed itself the Provisional IRA, found itself increasingly isolated as the support of the community waned, forcing it into relative inactivity.

Eventually, in 1969, the IRA focused its attention on the growing number of civil disturbances and the increasing discontent within the Belfast ghettos at the rising level of unemployment and the ever-increasing poverty. Seeing this as an opportunity to reopen the old wounds, they began a campaign of sectarian murder designed to cause retaliation and also to turn the populace against the authorities who, the IRA claimed, were deliberately not providing adequate protection for the people because British law and order was biased against the Catholic minority.

The Stormont government tried unsuccessfully to suppress the escalating murders, and soon turned to Whitehall for an answer. However, across the Irish Sea the British government believed, albeit naively, that the sectarian killings would cease and normality return if the two warring factions were physically separated. But with the Royal Ulster Constabulary (RUC) stretched to near breaking point and no end in sight, the government chose a 'short-term' solution with the deployment of the army. Though at the time this seemed a feasible remedy to the problem, it later proved to be a fatal decision. The government's 'quick fix', which was supposed to last a maximum of six months, dragged on for a further 25 years. The army, though well trained and with unlimited access to finances, seriously lacked senior commanders with experience of urban conflict or, even as a minimum, an understanding of Irish history.

It came as no surprise when the army was turned from friend into foe in a matter of only a few weeks, its ranks becoming the target not only of public displeasure, but also of assassins' bullets. However, unlike their superiors, they were unable to request bodyguard protection, though a few would certainly end their careers employed as such.

The principal aim of the Provisional IRA was always deliberately kept simple: boot the British out of Ireland, a slogan that intentionally appealed to a much wider audience than those of the past. Soon after the protest marches began and the sectarian murders continued, the Provisional IRA wasted no time in beginning its campaign of terror, starting with the random sniping and bombing of passing army patrols and progressing to the selected political assassination of prominent VIPs, exploiting the lax security. Northern Ireland soon became the world's number one VIP killing zone, closely followed by Germany and Italy.

In public, Western governments implemented a two-pronged attack using both 'preventive' and 'reactive' capabilities. The former was the passive response to terrorism, using intelligence from covert surveillance operations to lead to the arrest and conviction of active members, while the latter was the aggressive response, the deployment of armed units with the declaration of a readiness to kill if attacked.

Up to this point bodyguards had always been regarded as solitary figures working solely to keep their principal out of danger. Rarely did they have access to, or even carry, firearms. In fact, even if bodyguards had opted to use weapons, the rule of law in many countries governing their carriage nearly always restricted their use, often to an extent that made them all but useless. Some bodyguards, as has been seen, preferred and often resorted to physical violence to protect their clients. Yet almost overnight bodyguards became, in theory at least, part of Europe's aggressive response, and under a government-sponsored umbrella they were allowed, for the first time in history, the right to return fire and lawfully kill those who stepped from the shadows with the intention of assassination. Suddenly bodyguards were catapulted to the forefront of Europe's defence against the international terrorist assassin, and became powerful tools for their political masters to parade on all public occasions.

However, VIPs were a long way from total safety, and many gave their lives before governments realised that bodyguards could only be used to deter or defend, not to defeat terrorism. That was the domain of an agency not yet in place.

Outside the sphere of personal protection, little was achieved in forming the 'preventive' or 'reactive' capability by the autumn of 1972. This was due to the lack of political direction regarding whether the state police or its military big brother should provide the aggressive response. This was never going to be an easy question to answer, even if it did seem a simple one on the surface. Underlying considerations had to be resolved before a firm commitment could be made to either force. In the United Kingdom, for instance, the arming of the police was a controversial subject that had no public support, and was further compounded by the majority of police officers being against the idea of bearing arms. In Italy and Germany the decision in favour of the police was easily made, but led to interdepartmental rivalry and arguments over which faction of the police force was best qualified to supply the units. There was also a growing lobby of politicians from many countries who believed that the use of police officers, with the likelihood of shooting to kill, overstepped their powers of law enforcement, and asserted that the aggressive function should be left in the hands of those best qualified, the military. However, state governments saw the deployment of military élite units on to the streets as an open admission that they were unable to control the terrorist problem and, in the worst scenario, led to the collapse of basic law and order and an escalation in criminal activity. Although this statement could not be justified on closer inspection, many governments stuck to it.

Such squabbles only clouded the already murky waters and delayed the implementation of security measures to prevent activists from every corner of the globe continuing their campaign of terror and violence. Not surprisingly perhaps, politicians and diplomats conveniently ignored the fact that bodyguards from military élite units like the SAS were already training overseas protection teams in anti-terrorist techniques, and many state police forces had officers working in the 'reactive' role as personal protection officers.

As events would have it, the dithering came to an abrupt halt in September 1972, when eleven Israeli athletes were slaughtered during a gun battle between members of the 'Black September' terrorist movement and untrained German security forces at Munich Airport. The massacre unfolded live on the television screens of a worldwide audience of 500 million people, and the inability of Western security forces to deal with the threat of terrorism was exposed in the bloodiest manner to the world's mass media. The British government, shocked and stunned by the incident, immediately instructed the SAS to develop its own counter-terrorist capability, and injected unlimited funds to purchase the best equipment and facilities available. The regiment, under the command of Lieutenant Colonel (later Brigadier General) Peter de la Billiere, helped by Lieutenant Colonel Anthony Pearson, set about widening its almost non-operational Counter Revolutionary Warfare (CRW) Wing into a fully deployable force. First the regiment had to find experienced soldiers trained in counter-terrorist techniques and with operational experience, but there were not too many about at the time. Commanders quickly turned to the regiment's small but active bodyguard training team.

The unit was formed in 1967 during a lull in SAS operational commitments, and in direct response to rumours that an amalgamation was on the cards in the impending defence review. Regimental officers realised at the time that, with no wars to keep its soldiers busy and only a small contingent of troopers on operational duties, they had to look elsewhere to justify their existence. The creation of a specialist unit dedicated to providing personal protection, with the ability to compensate for the increasing number of Third World assassinations, seemed a viable solution. But the training team, manned by a small cadre of four long-serving soldiers and under the direct administrative control of the Operations and Intelligence Wing, were rarely seen in barracks; their almost endless trek around the hemisphere conducting two-week protection courses saw to that.

Initially the team's training was conducted on inadequate ranges using outdated equipment, but with the arrival of the additional resources in 1972, and the team's recall from Uganda, the unit was able to update its Close Quarter Battle (CQB) House, or 'Killing House' in SAS jargon, to accommodate not only its bodyguards but later its famous black-clad Hostage Rescue Teams. The CQB House was primarily designed to train rookie bodyguards in the skills of shooting assassins in confined places without hitting innocent bystanders, but with governments preoccupied with the increasing threat of hostage situations, the emphasis was changed in 1975 to train Hostage Rescue Teams in the same basic principles but to a much higher standard. This idea proved so successful during the Iran embassy siege in 1980 that the CQB House, in many different forms, has since been adopted by over 50 countries worldwide. The original set-up in Hereford has since been updated and is now equipped with the most sophisticated 'virtual reality' wrap-around screen technology available; technology that does not require the teams to fire live rounds, and therefore reduces the number of injuries from ricochets which dogged training teams in the beginning.

At about the same time the Australian SAS was also playing its part in protecting VIPs in the southern hemisphere. Its small cadre of bodyguards provided personal protection for numerous leaders in the Far East, and in response to Britain's creation of the CRW Wing the Australian regiment did the same soon after returning from the Vietnam war.

The British government's continued enthusiasm for the development of a CRW Wing allowed the regiment to expand its operational base further, into the dangerous world of hostage rescue and the specialist area of undercover surveillance operations. The addition some years later of the Operational Research and Development (ORD) Wing, dedicated to the acquisition and testing of new equipment not available on the open market, was a major step forward, not only for the regiment, but for British bodyguards in general.

Today the CRW Wing supports a full bodyguard training and advisory team (depending on regimental commitments) that has helped groom and cultivate a number of agencies, including instructors from the Royal Military Police Bodyguard Training School and personal protection officers from Special Branch's 'A' Squad. Every few years the Wing also provides one-off refresher courses for members of the Royal Family to 'acclimatise' them to the possibility of assassination, and on the rare occasion when the Special Branch considers a target to be so 'hypersensitive' that additional cover is required, the Wing will supply its best marksmen to bolster the protective blanket. This occurred in London during the 50th anniversary celebrations of VE Day, when two troops of SAS marksmen, along with armed officers from the Royal Marine Commandos and covert surveillance teams from military intelligence, were deployed to provide a covert protection screen around two visiting VIPs, King Hussein of Jordan and the Vice-President of the USA, Senator Al Gore.

Other Western nations similarly disturbed by the Munich massacre ordered the creation of their own specialist anti-terrorist units based on the British SAS but preferring Germany's decision to use selected police officers, a decision that created the GSG9. Austria, with its small population and limited resources, formed a scaled-down version, the Cobra, which received much of its training from GSG9. France initially developed the Compagnies Républicaines de Securité (CRS), although after some internal feuding about their professionalism the Groupe d'Intervention de la Gendarmerie Nationale (GIGN) took over the responsibility of all international anti-terrorist operations. The Spanish continued on the same theme with the Grupo Especial de Operaciones (GEO), while the Italians developed the Nucleo Operativo Centrale di Sicurezza (NOCS) on similar lines, and with the help of the Israeli Sayaret Matkal. Although there were similarities between these units and the SAS, there remained one fundamental and abiding difference; the SAS was the only unit manned, and trained, by soldiers, although the GIGN did later second military personnel into its ranks to bolster its experience for specialist clandestine operations.

America followed the mainstream of European countries and incorporated its counter-terrorist capability into its federal police force, mainly by expanding and retraining its Special Weapons and Tactics (SWAT) teams in anti-terrorist techniques, though they proved of limited use and were supplemented sometime later by the Critical Incident Response Teams (CIRT), under the control of the FBI's Special Operations and Research Unit. The Bureau's Hostage Rescue Teams (HRT) were born from the need to rescue political targets from the hands of terrorists, especially if they were visiting diplomats the USA refused to sacrifice. Nevertheless, soon after the GSG9 rescue at Mogadishu in 1977, American military commanders recognised that the HRTs were limited in their powers to deal with incidents outside the USA, and that the country had no effective capability to deal with a hostage rescue in a situation like that at Mogadishu. To resolve the problem, Colonel Charles Beckwith (who had served with the British SAS in the early 1960s) was ordered to establish the counter-terrorist unit Delta Force, with the responsibility of all hostage rescues outside the USA's frontiers. The unit soon emerged as an exact replica of the SAS CRW Wing, and in fact its first military recruits were trained by the SAS in Britain. The regiment also helped build the unit's first 'House of Horrors', based on the 'Killing House' in Hereford.

These units gave governments two advantages: firstly the ability to supply highly trained bodyguards for selected VIPs on short secondments, and secondly the ability to rescue hostages from the hands of determined killers while saving the authorities the embarrassment of giving in to terrorist demands. Today, bodyguarding has come full circle in its evolution. These units initially established Europe's capability to meet the threat of international terrorism, and from them have been drawn today's military and civilian personal protection officers. Even government bodyguards are trained by, or originate from, Hostage Rescue Teams.

Because of their sophisticated training and the immense firepower at their disposal, anti-terrorist units can only be used in the most exceptional circumstances, and normally only after the police authority has admitted that negotiations have failed or that the lives of the hostages are in immediate danger. Even at that point, authority for their use has to be gained from the highest political level.

Governments were not slow to realise that the use of such anti-terrorist forces could probably incur a high number of hostage casualties, and they agreed in private that they should be used only as an absolute last resort. But even with the 'curative' response in place, governments still needed to improve their 'preventive' capability, to ensure that police forces detected and arrested wanted terrorists before they could implement their plans. Normal police channels had proved futile when dealing with the problem because forces were limited in their geographical area of operations, and the problem was further complicated by the fact that terrorism had origins outside the forces' lawful jurisdiction. What was required was a European centralised criminal data processing and surveillance unit. Interpol (the International Police), with its worldwide web of offices and its constant cross-flow of criminal data, was just what the experts were calling for. However, Interpol was an organisation aimed at detecting and arresting those involved in criminal rather than political activity, and its commanders refused to allow the agency to be used in the investigation of any crime relating to terrorist acts of violence.

As politicians and experts argued over what should be done to bring Interpol back into line, Germany went its own way to solve the problem with action rather than words, and inadvertently led the way for the rest of Europe by reorganising the Bundes-Kriminal-Amp (BKA, or Federal Criminal Office) to provide a centralised database. This was not a new idea, but the BKA also incorporated specially trained 'Target Teams' to gather intelligence. This approach was new only regarding the way in which the giant intelligence puzzle was pieced together. With each team dedicated to tracking just one suspect at a time, they were able to collate information that much quicker, and any information pertaining to another terrorist was quickly passed directly to the relevant surveillance team rather than to the central database, and vice versa. This system drastically cut, but did not eradicate, the need to maintain a time-consuming index-card system used by many of the world's intelligence agencies. The approach also reduced the likelihood of a vital piece of the jigsaw puzzle being lost within thousands of index-cards, never to resurface. Being able to concentrate efforts on watching the target led to an arrest rate that was unmatched elsewhere. The BKA's only drawback was its refusal to share information with other European states, but despite this it proved so successful that it broke the back of the most ruthless terrorist organisation in German history, the Baader Meinhof gang.

The agency's relentless determination in the pursuit of wanted terrorists knew no bounds. This was demonstrated in 1978 with the arrest of four wanted terrorists in a Black Sea holiday resort in Bulgaria, followed by their prompt, but secret, flight back to Cologne to await trial, an idea that was adopted by the American government and became its official policy in 1989. The start of the 1980s saw the BKA celebrating its positive identification of 65 active members of the Baader Meinhof gang, many of whom were either killed or awaiting trial. Those few who remained at large continued making only small, insignificant attacks that received little or no publicity.

Britain and America watched with interest as the BKA rounded up terrorist after terrorist, and soon set about developing their own intelligence and surveillance teams. British intelligence officers working in Northern Ireland during this period admitted they had next to no intelligence on Republican paramilitary organisations. In an attempt to rectify this, MI5 and military intelligence set up covert agent-running networks to infiltrate terrorist organisations in the hope of gaining advance warning of future assassinations. Simultaneously, on the mainland, Scotland Yard developed its own anti-terrorist branch based on BKA principles but with the addition of a Bomb Squad manned by experts from the military's bomb disposal teams, an idea that was to reap unprecedented rewards a decade later but had no immediate effect. The odds of defeating Irish terrorism were always stacked against the counter-terrorist units, especially after the Provisional IRA abolished its military-style structure in favour of smaller Active Service Units (ASUs) which enhanced security and gave greater flexibility. This idea was quickly adopted by other European terrorist organisations, making the job of tracking and watching wanted terrorists all the more difficult.

It took some time for the multitude of counter-terrorist agencies operating in Europe to attain the same levels of competence, so that they could work together effectively to start the uphill struggle to defeat terrorism. However, in 1985 European terrorist organisations also combined forces in an attempt to stay one step ahead of the pursuers. In a joint declaration, two of the main players on the continent, the Action Direct movement and the Red Army Faction, warned of an increase in assassinations and bomb attacks on NATO targets. They were not lying. By the end of the year 51 serious attacks had been reported on a multitude of targets, including a massive explosion inside a US Air Force base at Frankfurt which killed two people and injured seventeen. This was followed soon after by the assassination of Gerold von Braunmuhl, a senior German Foreign Office official shot dead as he returned home. The weapon was later positively identified by BKA ballistic experts as the one that also killed Hans-Martin Schleyer.

While the new campaign of terror chalked up its successes, counter-terrorist units in Germany, Britain and Italy came under increasing pressure as their attempts to gather intelligence on the new 'third generation' of terrorists faltered. One of the knock-on effects of this, though it was not immediately apparent, was to deprive body-guards on the ground of the vital intelligence needed to keep VIPs 'out of harm's way', in Secret Service jargon.

Even the BKA, which had once been so successful, was now making no notable arrests, and accusations of incompetence and inefficiency were rife. In fairness, this could not have been further from the truth. Surveillance operations had identified a growing number of known terrorists openly living within France and Belgium, but because of political bureaucracy and ministerial mismanagement the BKA was restricted in its movements and the action it could take, and was effectively powerless to stop or deter future attacks. This was particularly the case while France maintained its long-standing tradition of granting asylum to exiles of any political persuasion, including those that resorted to terror to achieve their goals, in return for an unspoken agreement that they did not bring violence to the streets of Paris. However, extradition from France was a far greater problem than the knowledge that terrorists could attack without hindrance, and even though many countries attempted extradition throughout the 1970s and early 1980s they were hampered by France's blatant refusal to extradite on the grounds that, 'offenses relating to political conduct would, if tried in another country, not result in a fair trial'.

Although this might have been a controversial issue, France was not the only continental country which refused to extradite. Germany continually refused to hand over Mohammed Hamadei to the FBI for his part in the killing of Robert Stetham, a US Navy diver shot in the head during the hijacking of Flight TWA 847 in 1987 and unceremoniously dumped on the tarmac in full view of the world, despite the fact that the FBI provided 'substantial proof' that Hamadei was the Islamic Jihad leader in charge of the operation.

Although countries have an international legal duty to extradite, and bilateral treaties have been ratified by members of the European Economic Community, the ultimate decision remains with the holding government. Extradition today is not the highly contentious issue it once was, and many nations abide by the 'compromise' treaties and agreements that allow terrorists to be tried in the holding state, but with the evidence gathered by a multitude of external agencies. Much of this evidence can come from an array of sources, including the FBI's National Crime Information Center (the USA's equivalent of the BKA), computerised telephone intelligence ('phone tapping) and electronic surveillance (the use of authorised bugs to gather foreign counterintelligence). These sources are only the tip of a massive intelligence iceberg now in place across Europe and the USA, much of which is still shrouded in secrecy and mystery, and to which government protection agencies also have access.

In response to the new breed of 'Euro-Terrorism', bodyguards modified their own capability of preventing the assassin from getting 'too close'. Protection teams knew from experience that the professional killer, terrorist or otherwise, preferred to live to fight another day by using stand-off technology: the sleeper bomb or sniper fire. Close-range assassination is fast becoming a tactic of the past, used as a last resort and then only if an escape route is available. The bodyguards' ability to identify and cut off these potential routes would cause assassinations to be aborted, and to achieve this goal, protection team leaders quickly adopted covert counter-surveillance teams placed either at the rear of crowds or, where necessary, moving along in line with the VIP.

The US Secret Service had been using covert 'watchers' since the late 1950s, and although they were absent during the presidential assassination of 1963, their numbers have flourished and their use has proved highly effective, so much so that the vast majority of governmental protection agencies in the world now incorporate undercover protection teams within their ranks. One highly placed bodyguard with ten years' experience of covert close protection work said mockingly: 'Things are not always as they seem'.

Personal protection officers also began to enhance their expertise in devising detailed contingency and emergency evacuation plans for the potential attack, based on what the assassin might do next rather than what he had done in the past. This worked to some degree to protect VIPs, but not to the extent that closer co-operation between bodyguards and the intelligence services was achieving. Sensitive information that once would not have been released to outside agencies was now finding its way to VIP security teams. This included the identification of known terrorists, their movements and, more importantly, their current whereabouts. Additional snippets of information pertaining to the transportation or collection of weapons and explosives was also provided. This meagre but vital information allowed trained bodyguards to make calculated guesses as to the likely place of the attack and, more importantly, gave early warning of the form it would take. Having the ability to identify potential target areas was indispensable in steering the VIP away from danger, and gave bodyguards greater flexibility and control when advising VIPs about future engagements.

All this new-found expertise was put to good use when one personal protection team provided the break that led to the arrest of the highly effective active Provisional IRA cell working on the Continent during the late 1980s. Their ruthless campaign had killed a number of British soldiers, including Major Michael Dillon-Lee, shot dead as he left his home in Dortmund, and two Australian tourists, Nick Spanos and Stephen Melrose, mistaken for British soldiers and killed as they returned to their parked car in Roermond. Europe's best anti-terrorist police officers had been trying to track down the IRA cells for months, and although they had arrested Gerard Hanratty and Terence McGeough in September 1988 for their part in the bomb attack on the British military headquarters in Rheindahlen the previous year, the attacks intensified.

Initial intelligence had suggested that the remaining members of the ASU had moved from their safe house in Sweden to another outside the border town of Cologne, but anti-terrorist police were unable to identify the house positively, or any members of the unit at a suspected building under covert surveillance. The building later turned out to have no connection with any terrorist group. Meanwhile in Britain, Scotland Yard mounted surveillance operations on potential IRA targets, including at least 200 VIPs, an operation that led directly to the arrest of Nessan Quinlivan and Pearse McAuley near the historic site of Stonehenge. They were later charged with conspiring to murder former Whitbread chairman Sir Charles Tidbury.

Fearing for the lives of top military commanders in the light of the ASU activity, the Ministry of Defence deployed extra Royal Military Police bodyguards to protect those most at risk. One of these bodyguard teams providing protection for a senior commander noticed two known IRA terrorists, Pauline O'Kane and Patrick Murray, watching their movements during a memorial visit to the Belsen concentration camp near Hanover in early July 1988. The protection team leader, a sergeant, immediately alerted military intelligence, who in turn informed the BKA. Within hours specialist surveillance teams had located the ASU, and over the next three weeks they painstakingly followed them before finally surrounding them at a wood near the Belgian border. Ironically, the wood had already been positively identified some months earlier by Belgian police as containing an arms dump. However, the surveillance operation had been called off after weeks of inactivity, and an Armalite rifle in the cache was 'jarked' (a bugging device was concealed inside the weapon). This operation, which included the removal of the weapon's firing pin, was carried out under the cover of night by officers flown in from the Weapons Intelligence Unit of the British Army in Northern Ireland.

At the moment the ASU was attempting to test the weapons, anti-terrorist officers from both operations swooped into action, and after some initial confusion Pauline O'Kane and Patrick Murray were arrested. Some days later Donogh O'Kane and Donna Maguire were also arrested in the Irish Republic as they boarded a ferry bound for England. Sources within military intelligence have told the author that the identities of the continental ASU members were known well in advance of their arrest, and that the commander, Pauline O'Kane, was the suspected escaped 'fifth member' of an ASU that was shot dead in Gibraltar by the British SAS in 1988 (the 'fourth member' escaped to New York but was later extradited). After escaping death, O'Kane had travelled north to meet up with three other members. Two of the three, Hanratty and McGeough, were later arrested and replaced by Murray and Maguire, both of whom were followed to the airport by undercover soldiers. Pauline O'Kane replaced the ASU commander, John Corr, who was recalled to the Province to take command of the IRA in Coalisland, with the more important task of finding the police informer of the Loughall shooting the previous year. The IRA high command did not have to wait long. Less than a year later Corr and another IRA activist, Brian Arthurs, were stopped by RUC police officers and arrested for the abduction of Collette O'Neill, found bound and gagged in the back of the vehicle and on her way to interrogation and almost certain execution. She was immediately taken into protective custody and flown to Nottingham with a two-man SAS protection team.

After O'Kane took control of the continental ASU, the number of bombing and shooting attacks increased dramatically during that year. They started in May with the assassination of three off-duty Royal Air Force soldiers in the Netherlands, followed by two bomb blasts at Duisburg and Düsseldorf which injured thirteen, and the killing of Warrant Officer Richard Heakin, shot dead as he waited for a ferry in Ostend, France. The year 1989 saw no let-up in the campaign of killing, five bomb attacks and four shootings resulting in five deaths.

Although the newly arrested four denied all connection with terrorism, a large quantity of explosives and bomb-making equipment was found at flats rented by Donna Maguire and Pauline O'Kane in Belgium. But the most damning evidence lay not in the courtroom, but in the fact that the IRA's campaign of violence on the Continent suddenly came to an abrupt halt. Bodyguard counter-surveillance techniques had paid off.

Yet with the successes in Europe there came failures in the Province itself. Security forces had been attempting to corrode the Provisional IRA from within for many years, the most notable example being with the use of 'supergrasses' to provide valuable intelligence to convict their fellow brothers-in-arms. Using supergrasses was not a new idea; the Italian police had perfected the art and proved it to be a workable solution with the conviction of numerous organised crime godfathers long before it became the official policy of the British government. Statistically, the policy proved very successful for the RUC. A total of 27 terrorists turned 'state's evidence' which led to the conviction of 590 people. However, many of those convicted on the evidence of supergrasses alone were later released on appeal owing to growing doubts about the validity of the information they provided and the effect of incentives offered in return for that information, which included immunity from prosecution, a new life and identity overseas, and heavy cash rewards.

The personal protection of supergrasses in Northern Ireland was in the hands of the SAS until its men were replaced by bodyguards from the RUC after the regiment was deployed to Dhofar in 1970. But contrary to official denials, the SAS did continue to provide protection for a select number of high-ranking informers considered to be at unusually high risk. Joseph Bennett, Kevin McGrady and Raymond Gilmour are known to have received the elaborate protection of their once bitter opponents.

The security precautions implemented the moment military bodyguards were assigned have never been revealed before. In the case of Gilmour it included his family's removal under the cover of darkness to a military base in Germany, before being flown by the Royal Air Force to the British Army Training unit in Suffield, Canada, where they remained in married quarters in a secluded part of the base. The 'family', with imposed guardians, did not have to wait long before they were on the move again after arrangements had been made with the American State Department (often through the Foreign and Commonwealth Office in London or Washington) for the provision of an apartment in exchange for the same facilities in the UK for one of its own informers. The Australian government is also known to have provided, and received, similar hospitality from both countries. Moreover, British bodyguards could obtain safe accommodation through the Foreign and Commonwealth Office in France, Germany, Cyprus, New Zealand and South Africa, to name but a few countries.

This cross-co-operation is not unusual today, but in the days when governments were embedded in sporadic love/hate relationships bodyguards conducted their own negotiations to borrow facilities through 'contacts' within the chosen country, and this certainly helped to keep the hindrance of diplomatic or political interference to a minimum.

The deliberate use of bodyguards to protect those who were to play a significant if short-lived part in the attempted defeat of the IRA was one of the first signs of the growing importance of bodyguards to their political masters. Irish terrorism often used the tools of assassination and abduction during its long campaign of terror against the British, and it was not only politicians who found themselves on the assassins' death list; prominent members of the judiciary also stepped involuntarily into the line of fire. This started in 1973 with the killing of Judge William Doyle on his way to mass; he had fatally dismissed his RUC bodyguard for the day. Despite the public outcry, the murder was soon superseded by the death of Belfast magistrate William Staunton as he collected his daughter from school in the Republican Falls Road of Belfast. The following year saw no improvement in the situation, with the killings of magistrate Martin McBirney, murdered at his East Belfast home, and Judge Rory Conahan, shot in the head as he answered his front door. However, the saddest event in this spate of killings was the shooting of William Travers and his young daughter, both sprayed with bullets as they left Sunday mass. Travers survived, but his daughter did not.

To eliminate such easy targets, the RUC issued a booklet aptly entitled *Personal Protection Measures*, advising that individuals should maintain 'a high degree of alertness when ... preparing to drive away ... opening the front door at night', and that 'all late night callers should be regarded as suspicious'. It added that, 'as 63 per cent of assassinations are instigated at night ... gardens should be well lit to deny the cover of darkness to a potential assassin'. The RUC also began the practice of consulting those who had agreed to be appointed to the high bench and, for those who were at the greatest risk, 10ft fences were erected around their homes, supplemented by close-circuit television cameras manned by a 24-hour RUC personal protection team. Those at the lower end of the scale could hope for no more than the occasional drive past of an RUC patrol or, on a rare occasion, the advice to carry a gun, for which a firearms licence was duly granted.

Nevertheless, the Provisional IRA was renowned for adapting its tactics when 'soft targets' were no longer available, and soon the emphasis was back on political murder, with two bomb attacks on former Prime Minister Edward Heath soon after he lost the 1974 general election and, simultaneously, his bodyguard protection (this was reinstated some weeks later). The first bomb, thrown on to a balcony of his home in Wilton Street, London, caused serious damage to the building but no casualties. The second, some months later, was a more serious attempt on his life. A magnetic sleeper bomb was attached to the underside of his car but failed to detonate, falling harmlessly to the ground where it was diffused by military bomb disposal experts some hours later. A similar device, but with the addition of a sophisticated tilt switch, successfully killed MP Airey Neave as he drove up the exit ramp of Westminster car park five years later.

Financing overseas operations was never an easy task for the Provisional IRA, and as the 1980s came to a close, funds were depleting to worrying levels for the IRA high command, especially after Libya, Iran, Syria and Jordan stopped the flow of cash and arms following the collapse of the Soviet Union. Admittedly Moscow had never directly financed terrorism, but it had openly supported countries that did. Yet when the Soviet attitude changed towards *Perestroika* in an attempt to obtain billions of dollars in aid from the West, supporting international terrorism was the wrong way to go about getting it. No longer could countries that financed terrorism play the superpowers off against each other, and terrorism soon lost its appeal. The Gulf War also played a vital role in denting terrorist funds. Those countries in the region that was once bitterly opposed to Western governments, mainly because those Western governments, particularly America, supported Israel, were suddenly calling on them for military assistance to stop the tyrant Saddam Hussein from expanding his empire by force. The Arab leaders got what they wanted, but at the price of denouncing all forms of terrorism.

Despite these two global occurrences, one incident much closer to home hammered the last nail into the IRA's financial coffin. Two bombs were left in a busy shopping precinct in the centre of Warring-

ton in 1993, and 45 minutes after a coded warning had been telephoned to the Samaritans at 11.58 a.m., and while police officers were
still checking the area, the bombs exploded, killing a four-year-old
child and seriously injuring another as they were buying a Mother's
Day present. A further 54 people were hurt. Widespread public condemnation followed the killing as usual, but this time the murder of a
child on the streets of mainland Britain caused deep resentment not
seen in the country since the Birmingham pub bombings in 1977 and
the Enniskillen killings a decade later. It is impossible to gauge the disagreement within the high command in Belfast following the bombing,
or among the IRA's supporters in the Republican areas of Belfast, but
there can be no doubt that the IRA top brass had made a misjudgment
which lost the organisation a great deal of financial support, especially
from the Northern Aid Committee, commonly called Noraid.

Financial security and operational independence for the IRA was
not totally dependent on the funds received from America. In fact, up
to 1987 the Provisional IRA received approximately £4 million in total
from Noraid since the conflict had begun in 1969, compared with
three times that figure from its own use of extortion, protection rackets and armed robbery. Yet police anti-corruption units knew that
closing down the American financial connection would seriously
damage the IRA's effectiveness in mounting its operations in mainland
Britain. Nevertheless, Noraid was a registered company permitted
under US law to send funds to Ireland as 'relief', and officials, when
pressed by the British government to stop the funds, insisted there was
no evidence to connect Noraid relief funds 'with any organisation
advocating violence', despite the fact that Armalite rifles and pistols of
American manufacture had been seized in Northern Ireland and
directly linked to IRA sympathisers living in the USA.

With Noraid financial support untouchable, anti-corruption officers turned their attention to other sources of IRA funds: financial
extortion, protection rackets, video piracy and armed robberies. The
advantage the British police had over their European counterparts
during this period lay primarily in the undercover operations conducted by five separate agencies within the province. The British

intelligence service (MI5) had taken a long-term view at the start of the conflict, with their agents running networks which were now actively supplying crucial information. These covert agents quickly built up a picture of the IRA's extensive protection racket and extortion operations. Simultaneously, uniformed commanders expanded the 'anonymous free-call' telephone line that was proving successful in catching criminals and obtaining usable intelligence on terrorist-related activities.

Over the months, anti-corruption police using covert surveillance and wire-tapping had compiled a dossier of over 37 volumes on the Provisional IRA's use of extortion alone. Co-ordination of this information and its legality once arrests were made was critical to the success of the operation. When the operation was finally concluded and arrests began, in 1993, it succeeded in destroying the IRA's finances, even though it received barely a paragraph in many leading British newspapers. This operation, together with the increased success the RUC were having in intercepting armed robbers during raids, went a long way to ensure that paramilitary finances were drastically cut.

It appears that these two low-profile operations caused the IRA top brass to look elsewhere for a solution to its financial predicament. During 1993-4, funds received by the IRA had plummeted by 70 per cent, certainly helped by the end of the Cold War, forcing the Provisional high command to plan one last massive campaign of death and destruction in the hope of generating new backers. There followed a mortar bomb attack on Downing Street and massive explosions at military and civilian installations, killing both soldiers and civilians, but this was to be to be the IRA's last campaign, and failed to gain any new backers.

The terrorist hard-line leadership was finally forced to declare a ceasefire and begrudgingly pass the struggle for a united Ireland to their political wing, Sinn Fein. After 25 years of near civil war on the streets of Northern Ireland, the British had succeeded in reducing, but not eradicating, the threat from Irish terrorism. The irony is that the Provisional IRA had little effect on changing either the political structure or policies of successive British governments, and ultimately only succeeded in reducing the possibility of a united Ireland. Even within Republican areas, the majority of the population preferred a peaceful campaign to a violent struggle. The Irish people have shown commendable resilience towards violence. No matter how much death and destruction the terrorists created, they maintained the irrepressible attitude that 'life goes on', an almost identical motto to that of the bodyguard.

Overall, the effectiveness of worldwide counter-terrorist developments in the last ten years, undoubtedly helped by the collapse of the Soviet Union and its knock-on effect on countries that financed terrorism, has all but rendered the threat from terrorist assassination defunct. Despite this, bodyguard protection remains in great demand as international terrorism is superseded by local activists with much loftier visions. The World Trade Center and Oklahoma bombings, coupled with the gas attack on the Japanese underground in 1994-5, are clear signs of this, and, it can only be a matter of time before additional roots of insurrection sprout up across Europe and America to wreak their vicious hatred on the democratic world once again. Fortunately the capabilities to meet the threat are in place, unlike a decade ago, when much of the fight against terrorism had an almost *ad hoc* approach, often supported by crossed fingers and wishful thinking. For the professional bodyguard, paid to stand between life and death, there could be no such approach. Too much was at stake.

3

Stay Alert, Stay Alive

Assassinations last no more than three or four seconds, a maximum of five shots being fired. During this period the VIP's bodyguards are under immense stress, knowing that any hesitation will result in the death of their client. Preparing personal protection officers to shield the principal and ferry him to safety in this moment of chaos, when the body is frozen in shock, the heart is pounding, legs are shaking, the mind is panicking and the vision has blurred to a tunnelled, hazy black and white, is a fine art in itself. Reactions such as these are not uncommon or a sign of weakness, but a natural response to fear. Bodyguard training instructors must replicate this fear to ensure that, when the moment arrives, the personal protection officer will be able to make the critical decisions that will ensure the VIP's continued existence.

Realistic training scenarios give bodyguards the opportunity to learn from mistakes without putting people's lives at risk, while at the same time giving their superiors the opportunity to see if they can handle the stress the job will bring. Not all can; in fact very few will finally pass into the world of government protection.

The bodyguards we see on the nightly news broadcasts, standing protectively around a monarch, the President of the USA or Britain's Prime Minister, are the few that have proved they can handle the stress of protective duties. They have shown that they can remain calm and controlled and react with devastating accuracy to 'take out' the assassin. They are at the pinnacle of bodyguard protection.

This level of bodyguard proficiency is not achieved overnight, or even after an eight-week training course. It is the culmination of years of progressive training and protection assignments conducted in many of the world's hot spots. Getting to the top requires relentless determination, practical proficiency, personal professionalism and, above all, unlimited stamina. 'Bravery,' in the words of one bodyguard, 'is born from fear, or stupidity, and bodyguards aren't stupid.' Stress forms a vital component during the three-week selection period for

Scotland Yard's protection teams. Police officers from any of the provincial forces across the country have to volunteer for close protection duties, and only those who, in the eyes of their seniors, have shown the right competence and aptitude are released from normal police duties to attend the course.

The American Secret Service indulges in a much more exhaustive screening process lasting more than twelve months. Agents with a desire to enter the presidential guard are subjected to comprehensive checks including drug testing, lie-detector interviews and psychological screening. Apart from protecting the President, the Secret Service also investigates cases of counterfeiting and fraud, and crimes relating to credit card deception, all on behalf of the US Treasury, a legacy dating back to the American Civil War, when the agency was originally formed to investigate the importation of forged currency. The contrast between the two tasks could not be greater, and though many special agents pass between bodyguard and investigation duties, and bodyguards are seen almost nightly on our television screens, it is virtually impossible to link the two. Rick Bundy, an ex-presidential bodyguard now with the investigation division, is hardly recognisable with his unshaven appearance, tatty jeans and dirty tee-shirt as the smart, suited, alert figure standing behind President Bush some weeks previously.

Secret Service bodyguards will start their careers not with protective duties, but with the investigation division. Here they are trained as undercover special agents, and often infiltrate organised crime syndicates to gather intelligence. Covert operations of this kind naturally come with their own 'stress factor', and after completing operational tours many special agents relish the opportunity to work as White House bodyguards.

The training ground for all potential Secret Service bodyguards is situated two miles outside Beltsville in rural Maryland, surrounded by an idyllic landscape. Few passing drivers would notice the compound's existence but for the high electrified wire fence and ever-moving infrared closed-circuit television cameras. The wooded 500-acre site hides a multitude of indoor and outdoor ranges. Tucked away in one corner are the mock streets that double as firing ranges, where bodyguards are presented with a multitude of good guy/bad guy targets. Every window and doorway hides a secret that forces split-second decisions from the rookie officers. In the centre of the compound sits the main building, dwarfing the newly built lecture rooms and accommodation blocks, and garages housing the extensive collection of motorcade vehicles, from humble Chevrolets to armoured Cadillacs.

Micky Miller, the Special Agent in charge of training presidential bodyguards, explained the purpose of the training course: 'It goes without saying that, first and foremost, a White House bodyguard's job is to keep the protectee out of harm's way, at whatever cost.' He added: 'Here we only have a short period of time in which to smooth out the rough edges, teach discretion, mould tomorrow's presidential guard, and tailor those who are more used to working as a loner to working as part of a team again.'

From the moment the rookie bodyguards arrive they are constantly kept busy. Days start before dawn and finish long after dusk. Fitness, firearms, first aid and fieldcraft can be followed by lectures on bomb countermeasures, combat survival or electronic surveillance, and if they have had an especially tiring day they will be given complicated mathematical problems to solve. Presidential bodyguards need to be able to think clearly even when totally exhausted. Trainees are given intense firearms training, using an array of weapons including the 9mm Glock handgun, the Uzi and the Heckler & Koch submachine pistol, and they also become proficient in the use of shotguns. Each student has to pass the Secret Service's marksmanship test under stress, a test that is not for the novice. To achieve the required standard, students will be required to spend hours on the ranges, expending in excess of 5,000 rounds. Trainee bodyguards can also make use of the Firearms Automated Training System, a relatively new piece of technological hardware for the Secret Service. This equipment was first tested and approved by the FBI in the early 1990s, and the Secret Service immediately saw its potential for honing the skills of the presidential bodyguard, at much reduced cost.

The trainees are locked in a small room in which they are surrounded by a wrap-around screen on to which a computer projects any number of real-time scenarios. The bodyguard is informed of his position relative to the VIP and other members of his protection team. The list of scenarios is endless, but the ending is always predictable, as the bodyguard knows there will be an assassin waiting in the crowd. If he reacts too slowly or hits bystanders, the screen freezes and a message appears. Protection officers have to be able to fire with pinpoint accuracy even if they are injured or carrying a VIP to safety. There is no room for error. Using the Firearms Automated Training System in conjunction with range practice certainly has its advantages; bodyguards can be tested in a multitude of 'real-time' situations not possible any other way. But it also has its disadvantages. In the words of Micky Miller: 'It's difficult to induce the "stress factor" or create fear inside a simulated box. The agent expects to be shot at, and is rarely wrong.' He continued: 'You cannot duplicate the recoil of a weapon or its malfunction at a critical time, both of which would certainly have an effect on how the bodyguard reacts.'

Skill at arms has to be of the highest standard when the course progresses to teaching firing techniques in close-quarter battle scenarios. Here bodyguards will be firing live rounds in dangerously close proximity to each other, not only inside buildings but from moving and static vehicles. There is no forgiveness for careless handling, particularly when they will be expected to return fire through a windscreen without hitting their passengers. This tactic was used to great effect during the attempted assassination of Antonio da Empoli, Italy's Finance Minister, as he stepped from his car to buy a newspaper. He instinctively ducked as the firing began, and his chauffeur, sitting at the wheel, returned fire through the passenger's side window, killing the female assassin.

Bodyguards, including those on this course, have the responsibility of bearing high-powered weapons in crowded civilian streets, and in untrained hands such weapons could cause catastrophic injuries and untold political damage. By its very nature the job requires mature, confident and unflappable personalities. Personal protection teams, regardless of where they are trained, must be fully conversant with the laws governing the carriage of firearms in the countries in which they will work.

However, government bodyguards working within known hostile areas such as Bosnia, Beirut, the Lebanon or Latin America would be unwise not to carry firearms openly. The blatant display of maximum firepower in areas notorious for assassination and abduction is the only way to deter an attack. On the other hand, bodyguards working in Britain or the USA are not permitted to carry firearms openly; in fact to do so would be counter-productive.

The training of top-level bodyguards in weapons handling is often accompanied by 'live' demonstrations of the lethal effect bullets have on the human body, and the use of human cadavers or live animals by bodyguard training teams is not uncommon. This ruthless but effective form of training matures would-be bodyguards and deliberately ensures that they think twice before going for their weapons.

Evasive driving skills are taught in the battered old Chevrolets, progressing to the armoured presidential limousine. As the air is filled with the sound of screeching brakes and the smell of burning rubber, the trainees practise reverse flick turns and anti-ambush drills. Handbrake turns are, in the words of one instructor, 'best left to Hollywood, because in real life they just don't work'.

There are practical drills to be learnt, too, including embussing and debussing a VIP from the vehicle, public walkabouts, and official engagements. A great deal of time will be spent on these practical lessons, but just as much time is devoted to classroom lectures.

Protection officers tend to be extremely taciturn especially in the presence of the press, and from 'day one' they learn to adopt a low profile. Peripheral skills taught on the course allow the bodyguard to build his personality so as to appear as just another guest at official engagements, so that rarely will he receive a second glance. 'We try to teach people how to behave, talk and eat correctly when in the company of VIPs. The last thing we need is for them to start eating their *gnocchi alla Romana* with their fish fork.'

Also part of the overall curriculum are surveillance and anti-surveillance techniques. The trainees are taught the importance of remembering the repeating face in a crowd, or those who pay undue attention to the close-protection team rather than the VIP. Public appearances by VIPs are rare but joyous occasions, and bodyguards quickly become suspicious of spectators who appear to be uncomfortable or up-tight, because professional assassination teams watch and record their victim's movements for months in advance to identify patterns and routines, often using reconnaissance teams that are just as highly trained in counter-surveillance techniques as the bodyguards they watch. However, there is a limit to the effectiveness of personal protection officers as far as counter-surveillance operatives are concerned. The bodyguards' main concern must always be the immediate danger to the VIP and removing him from potentially hazardous situations. The long-term threat must be left to others because counter-surveillance work requires very different skills to that of personal protection; skills that take years to master.

Security teams employed at the highest level always incorporate a specialist team to act as covert watchers and so cover all the angles. There is no shortage of men and women prepared to stand in someone else's killing zone, especially within the United Kingdom. Just as the US Secret Service is the pinnacle of American personal protection, the Special Branch 'A' Squad has a formidable reputation as the best bodyguards Europe can offer. Because they are assigned to protect only those deemed to be under the greatest threat, their selection and training has to be of the highest standard. Only the most motivated and dedicated police officers can enter such an élite unit, and rarely will they be below the age of 35, though this rule is flexible and some remarkably gifted young officers have joined the group.

There is a distinct *esprit de corps* within the unit and, unlike the Secret Service, which only allows its special agents to remain on presidential guard duty for a maximum of five years, Scotland Yard's 'A' Squad and the Royalty and Diplomatic Protection Group allow their officers to remain until retirement. Senior officers in control of the group see this as a way to maintain the balance between experience and the novice, because with pay in the private sector twice as high as in the police force there is always a need for constant supply of new blood. The training course for the Royalty and Diplomatic Protection Group is identical to that for their counterparts across the Atlantic.

However, much of the course is conducted 'out of house' with a private security company.

Physical endurance, especially upper-body strength, is vital to a protection officer. In time of trouble he must be able to carry the VIP to a waiting car while in full control of his senses and faculties. Often self-determination to succeed is all that will drive him on. The average age of Special Branch bodyguards is far higher than those in other worldwide protection agencies, including the Secret Service, where the average age is closer to 28, but having older bodyguards does not guarantee a better security screen, and in some cases can actually hamper it.

The course culminates in a realistic exercise lasting seven days at a nearby country house. Here the bodyguard hopefuls are put through their paces and everything that can happen does happen. For the nervous trainee there is no escape from the watchful eyes. Every room, corridor and hallway is fitted with hidden cameras and microphones; even the garden and vehicles are bugged. This is crunch time. Every mistake will be analysed by a team of critical bodyguards asking themselves the same question: could I work with this man? In this complex game of bluff and counter-bluff there is no time for relaxation. The attack may come at any time, from any direction. To the trainees an assassin lurks behind every tree and in every shadow, and as he patrols the grounds he hardly notices how picturesque the house looks surrounded by dense woodland and man-made lakes.

As the days progress the stress mounts. Lack of sleep leads to loss of concentration and countless false alarms. The protection team carefully accompanies the VIP as he goes about his daily routine, and an intimacy develops between guardian and guarded that is not always beneficial to protective cover. The trainee quickly learns that he is fighting an uphill struggle to attempt to sway his principal away from potential trouble. VIPs in a position of considerable power often show a blatant disregard for their own safety – until an attack begins.

Special Forces personnel often play the role of 'assassin', watching, waiting. When the attack comes it is ferocious. The air is filled with smoke and the smell of cordite. Gunfire can be heard from outside as hooded 'terrorists' try desperately to gain entry to the house.

The enemy does not obey the rules and the protection team is faced with an agonising decision; stay and fight, or make a break for it. The battle rages closer, the explosions are heard in the distance and CS gas wafts down corridors. The VIP is bustled into a waiting car by the team as others fight a withdrawal amid the hysteria inside the house. Within seconds the flying gravel and screeching tyres are an indication that the VIP has disappeared into the safety of the night. For those who successfully complete the course the door opens to the dangerous and unpredictable world of VIP protection.

Although the Secret Service and Scotland Yard are proud of their reputations, facilities and quality of protection, they resent any intrusion by the media. This resentment is not without foundation. The agency has often been accused of being a 'Praetorian Guard' which 'threatens to underpin democracy'. Some journalists have even gone so far as to say that they are 'arrogant and presumptuous', and during the US President's Whitewater scandal and the British Royal Family's recent marriage troubles, personal protection officers from both sides were approached, on an informal basis, by eager journalists hoping for an inside story. But as one royal protection branch bodyguard told the author: 'To think that we would tell tales or betray our clients' trust disgusts me to the core. Yes, we are loyal to the Royal Family, and yes, we are affected by Fleet Street stories, especially when they concern the relationships between us and members of the Royal Family. The very nature of the job requires us to be the VIP's confidante. We are there for one reason, and one reason only, to protect the individual.' He was referring to a newspaper report in Britain soon after the separation of Prince Charles and Princess Diana, which claimed that Diana's bodyguard was being more of a father to Prince William and Harry than Charles. The personal protection officer concerned was subsequently returned to normal police duties.

The Secret Service are not so candid about their feelings, but shrug off accusations of arrogance and presumptuousness with the universal comment: 'They have obviously never met us.'

In the world of VIP protection, all governments' security agencies now employ three layers of protection: personal protection officers, who are never out of arm's reach; close protection officers, sometimes referred to as covert bodyguards, whose task is to mingle with the crowd and identify threats or cut off escape routes; and the outer cordon, manned by uniformed police officers from the local force and providing the sole visual deterrent. Only government agencies have the resources available to carry out such security measures. For example, in the USA the Presidential Guard uses a hard core of twelve personal protection officers and thirty-six close protection officers, and the outer cordon can number in excess of two hundred. In the United Kingdom and Australia the Prime Ministerial cordons are not so top-heavy, but Britain's Prime Minister has a personal protection team of eight and a close protection team of four. Outside London, however, depending on the city to be visited, the latter figure could be tripled.

Protection officers will arrive weeks, sometimes months, before a visit to identify exactly where the exits and entrances are, where the VIP will stand, for how long, and what security precautions have already been taken by the local police or the venue's host. At this early stage they can also plan and check a safe approach route and emergency escape routes. Arrangements will be made for a safe room where the VIP can be taken if danger presents itself. Every venue must have a safe room equipped with a two-way radio, a secure telephone, emergency medical equipment and the VIP's personal doctor. The threat from bombs is no longer taken lightly, and it would not be unusual for the team to insist on inspecting the public elevators the VIP may or may not use. The working machinery, weights, counterweights, cables and shaft walls will be checked before they are closed to the public.

All bodyguards, no matter where they are trained, will be trained in identifying potential bomb threats. The sophistication of the 'improvised explosive device', in military jargon, has advanced in parallel with technology, and nowadays the art of bomb construction is limited only by man's ingenuity. The flexibility a bomb can give makes it the most used weapon of assassination in modern times. An expert can conceal a bomb inside anything from a cigarette carton to a lorry, and the advent of mouldable explosives such as Semtex has made bombs easier to conceal, and detection a job for specialist units. Protection officers receive a basic 'introductory' training, but this is swayed more towards the horrific injuries bombs can cause rather than their detection.

The devastating effect of explosions is brought home to bodyguards during lectures by bomb disposal officers with experience in Northern Ireland, Beirut and the Lebanon, and reinforced by graphic and gruesome videos taken by anti-terrorist police investigators immediately after bomb explosions. Secret Service bodyguards have to sit through the harrowing ordeal witnessed immediately after the Oklahoma bomb blast of early 1995. There are no limits to the video's macabre content and descriptive detail. As the voice-over commentary states that victims standing within five feet of the 1,000lb bomb were instantly vaporised, the video pans across the blood spattered rubble, past a child's hand cemented to a second-floor wall teetering on the brink of collapse, leaving even the most hardened of agents shell-shocked.

If such videos do not motivate bodyguards to fear and respect bombs, nothing will. While some bodyguards may see death from the assassin's bullet as honourable, in the words of one bodyguard: 'There's no dignity in being blown to bits.'

One method of assassination that is rarely used, even by professional assassins, though it allows the perpetrator to remain undetected, comes in the invisible and odourless form of poison. If delivered correctly, and at the right time, poison can have a detrimental effect on the way democracy is governed, especially if it is administered not to kill, but to remove the victim from the seat of power long enough to sow doubt in the mind of the populace and cause unrest. Bodyguards are trained in a variety of counter-measures to prevent assassination by poison. During state functions and formal receptions personal protection officers stand eagle-eyed between kitchen and table, guiding waiters to random tables. The old protocol of systematically serving food by starting with the top table has long been abandoned. Even when VIPs are offered food or drink during visits, no matter how innocuous it may appear, they are advised not to consume it but to relinquish it to their personal protection officer, who will dispose of it to an aide.

Such elaborate security measures can go too far, as a visit by the Queen to Northern Ireland shows. One community centre she was due to visit asked if she would try some of the local soda bread. Her aides thought this a good idea, but Palace security advisers refused. The disagreement was only resolved after the Palace's head chef agreed to watch the baking of three identical loaves, and moments before her arrival a close protection officer chose one of the loaves, the remainder being given to eager members of the media. Such precautions may appear excessive, but with biological laboratories continually experimenting to find more efficient ways to kill, the idea of poisoning is not as fictional as it at first appears. In fact, it is known that both the KGB and CIA have used drugs which lead to renal cancer within nine months. The victims suffer a painful and prolonged death, giving the assassins time to move a sympathetic successor into a position to take power.

This type of assassination tool is not yet available to even the most advanced terrorist groups. But there can be no better way to embarrass or destabilise a government than to have its leader riddled with syphilis or, worse still, die of AIDS.

There is no limit to the ways in which a victim can he poisoned. A VIP who chews his pen or licks his fingers to turn a page is prone to the expert poisoner. Bodyguards cannot alter the social habits of a VIP, especially taking into account the fact that, when the VIP is within a secure area (his office or private quarters), his personal protection officers will not be on hand to guide him or vet every object in the room. Even if its use is unlikely, assassination by poison is still a serious threat.

Measures have been adopted to reduce the threat to acceptable levels. One problem area concerns the employment of new staff. Vetting new employees to work within royal or government dwellings is a time-consuming and detailed task, often undertaken by the country's intelligence services. Nevertheless, the protection officers bear the ultimate responsibility, and it is not unusual for them to conduct their own informal 'interview'. One protection officer explained: 'New staff always present a certain amount of anguish initially; a chat with them allows you to "get the feel" of them.' He paused, deep in thought, then said: 'You can usually tell when something doesn't add up.'

Some methods of assassination cannot be trained for or anticipated. Silenced weapons emit no sound or visible smoke, and so are almost impossible to locate. The first sign of an assassination using such a weapon is normally when the VIP has been hit, leaving the bodyguard powerless and unable to take defensive action. For the bodyguard this first shot is the most crucial, because it is the signal that an attack has begun. Once the shot has been fired the bodyguards need to react and get the VIP to safety. If the first shot has hit the VIP, it is still imperative to get him away. At this point it is apparent that all preventive measures have failed to deter the assassin. Now it is down to the bodyguards' precautionary procedures to stop a second bullet from killing the VIP.

The wearing of ballistic armour is now commonplace for the majority of world leaders. Although Bill Clinton and John Major both refuse to wear it, they would accept their protection teams draping bulletproof trench coats around them at the vital moment. In the words of a White House bodyguard present in Panama (see Chapter 4): 'You'll be surprised just how quickly they change their minds when the bullets are flying.'

The most widely used body armour is Kevlar, a weavable material that can be made into any style or shape of clothing from light-weight waistcoats to military-style flak jackets. The degree of protection, and the style used, would depend solely on the threat to the VIP. For example, it would be unwise for a VIP not to wear body armour in the form of a flak jacket in the former Yugoslavia or in some parts of Latin America. Failure to do so would certainly invite assassination. The opposite is true in many European countries, where the wearing of body armour would be considered by the people to be an admittance that anarchy was taking over.

Currently, body armour is classed in 'threat levels'. The majority of VIPs wear 'Type II' Kevlar armour which can stop any round up to an 0.357mm magnum at close range. Heads of state and government, on the other hand, are advised to use only the 'Type IV' body armour with the ability to stop a NATO 7.62mm round fired from within two feet. Ballistic armour, not surprisingly, has become one of the fastest selling products within the security industry. The research and development of new armour is advancing day by day.

Ballistic protection can come in a variety of forms, starting with the attaché case which can be used as a bulletproof shield and also carry additional firepower. There are transparent clipboards, bomb blankets and letter-bomb pouches. But the most innocuous looking of all types of personal protection comes in the form of sunglasses used by the majority of bodyguards and some VIPs, especially in the USA and the Middle East. These 'designer' glasses, made by the Jones Optical Company in America, not only help cover the bodyguards' twitching eyes, but can stop a 0.38 special fired from less than fifteen yards.

Bulletproof armour is playing an increasingly important part in VIP protection. Even as this chapter was being written, news was coming in of an unsuccessful attempt on the life of President Mubarak of Egypt in the Ethiopian capital, Addis Ababa. Mubarak's limousine was riddled with bullets when six gunmen opened fire with Kalashnikov rifles, and the thick armour plating and bulletproof glass undoubtedly saved his life. This was not the first attempt on the Egyptian President since he came to power in 1981; nor will it be the last.

The use of armour-plated vehicles has now made motorcade murder a rare event. Nevertheless, the main threat has never come while the VIP is inside the vehicle, but while he is entering or leaving it. Recent history has shown that attempted assassinations often, but not always, occur as the VIP is walking toward or away from his limousine. Presidents Ford, Nixon and Reagan were all shot at as they walked to their limousines. This short walk is referred to as the 'Golden Ten' by the Secret Service (ten being the number of seconds the walk takes). It is during this period that the protection team will deploy the greatest number of overt and covert bodyguards and be at its most vigilant. The slightest hint of trouble is radioed to the entire team, and the bodyguards will use an alternative exit. It is also at this point that the bodyguard steps from the VIP's shadow and, albeit reluctantly, stands in the glare of the world's media. He will not do so as an act of bravado, but as a necessity. Top-level bodyguards prefer to be the anonymous figures in the background rather than the news celebrities. However, public interest has made the ever-watchful figure in the background the new object of their curiosity, and on closer inspection the bodyguard is seen not to be clearly at ease with all the attention. But despite his personal feelings he must guide his principal through the throng of clicking cameras without delay or interference.

For many protection officers the feeling of being watched is never far from their ever-alert minds. In today's technologically advanced society bodyguards must assume they are being watched at all times, night or day, indoors or out. The optical devices currently available range in their sophistication from the basic passive night goggles through to the American starlight scope, and 'electronic surveillance' or 'bugging' devices also vary in their complexity. At the lower end of the scale is the 'Mic-Insert' bug, which takes only a few seconds to install and requires no batteries, no aerial and no maintenance. Even the bodyguard with the presence of mind to remove the telephone mouthpiece would be looking directly at it.

The 'room monitor' is another simple but effective 'bug'. It connects quickly to any available telephone line and can transmit conversations from the targeted room to anywhere in the world. Some devices do not require access to the victim's house, being set up via the telephone's external junction box. The 'bug' is totally undetectable to the untrained eye, and even telephone engineers have failed to spot it. The device is activated when the victim lifts the receiver.

This is only a brief insight into the vast array of bugging devices available both to government agencies and the professional killer. However, government agencies have access to a wider range of highly sophisticated gadgets, some of which can even be set up and activated from outside the country, making detection almost impossible. But for every listening device invented there are just as many able to locate and neutralise them. Bodyguards are regularly updated on new developments in the eavesdropping business, and now one of their primary roles is to sweep locations the VIP will visit for possible 'bugs'.

Western government protection agencies have always had a shortage of women to train as bodyguards, while many Middle Eastern leaders actively employ complete teams of female protectors. President Gaddafi of Libya, with his 'Daughters of Revolution', is one of these, though many suspect they are part of the leader's harem rather than his bodyguards. One reason for the shortage could be that personal protection has always been seen as a male-dominated profession. However, while the Secret Service and Scotland Yard rarely have a shortage of female volunteers, many fail the selection and training process because of practical rather than professional reasons.

Bodyguards are prone to spend a lot of time alone, living out of suitcases and staying in hotels. For a man this poses few problems, but for a woman, staying alone in a hotel in a hostile country, especially in the Middle East where sexual restrictions are widespread, can cause problems. There are also problems with clothing and changing; a man can wear the same dinner suit for days, but a woman would quickly stand out if she repeatedly wore the same dress to formal functions. Again, while a man can quickly slip into the lavatory to change, a woman does not have the time or the same facilities.

Weapons also pose a problem for women, particularly regarding concealment. Currently, the only female protection officer on operational duties with Scotland Yard uses an underarm shoulder holster, but this is not always practical and she is obliged to carry the pistol in a handbag. Weapons handling is another reason why women do not fare well on the bodyguard training course. This is due to a physical problem. A woman's hand is much smaller than a man's, and the handgrips on the Glock pistol are of a standard size more suited to a male hand. Senior officers admit that this can certainly put a woman at a disadvantage when it comes to qualifying as a protection officer.

Of the 2,100 Secret Service agents available for protective duties, only 115 are female. The shortage is much more acute in Scotland Yard's 'A' Squad, where only four of the 200 protection officers are women. In Britain no one has an answer to the female shortage, and senior officers and firearms instructors would be happier if more women came forward. However, instructors are not prepared to drop standards to hush the critics. In the words of one instructor: 'Yes, we do need more female volunteers to come forward. But, no, we will not lower our standards or, as some have suggested, go back to employing unarmed female bodyguards. That would, in my opinion, have a detrimental effect on the protection we provide VIPs.' He continued: 'Admittedly the shortage will never improve as long as there is the stereotypical attitude that protection is ostentatiously a male job. It is not. We need female protection officers more than we do male. However, if they cannot handle a weapon competently we just cannot pass them.'

Close-protection training teaches bodyguards that there is no such thing as the 'perfect protection'. Some heads of state claim otherwise, but they are normally dictators who rarely leave the confines of their presidential palaces. The fact remains that if any assassin really wants to kill a VIP he will; nothing will ever change that. However, the majority of assassins (putting to one side the Islamic fanatics) are not prepared to be captured or killed in the process, and this gives bodyguards an even chance.

Unlike dictators, the majority of democratic leaders who wish to remain in power must be seen to be accessible to the people. The use of bodyguards or being surrounded by protective police officers is no longer frowned upon by the populace. On the contrary, the people see it as a show of power and strength, and are more inclined to have confidence in a leader with both qualities. During the American presidential elections one of the candidates, Ross Perot, refused Secret Service protection and hired his own low-profile security. His intention was purely honourable; to show himself as a leader not under siege. However, he was criticised by the media for his casual attitude to his safety, and lost much credit with the electorate, eventually falling by the wayside. Many security experts claimed he would have achieved more had he accepted Secret Service protection.

Grooming tomorrow's protection officers takes years. As a veteran instructor from the SAS told the author: 'A bodyguard is only as good as the knowledge he holds in his head. Knowledge that is accumulated over years of working across the world. Gut instinct, realistic training and advanced intelligence information are the keys that unlock the door to superior protection.' Today it is the politicians of the world who are increasingly likely to need that protection.

4

'Get Down, Mr President!'

As Hendrik Verwoerd, Prime Minister of South Africa, sat talking qui-etly to his Minister of Interior on the front bench of the House of Assembly in Cape Town during the fall of 1966, Demitrio Tsafendas, dressed in the distinctive uniform of the parliamentary messenger, stepped forward and stabbed the leader three times in the throat and heart. His party colleagues hardly noticed as the Prime Minister fell bleeding to the floor and died moments later.

Politicians are unique insofar that they can influence the course of events, and as a rule their murders are always motivated for politi-cal, religious, criminal, financial, psychopathic or racial gains. In the course of history many of the world's leaders have succumbed for one of the above reasons. Yet the killing of Verwoerd was no political assassination, and bore no racial motivation in a land where whites ruled blacks with an iron fist. In fact the killer was a notorious schiz-ophrenic, driven by the belief that his body was controlled by a large tapeworm. How he came to be employed as a parliamentary messen-ger defied logic and still raises eyebrows within the security industry.

American congressional members, worried about a similar attempt on the President, asked the Secret Service if the President was open to the same risk. The answer they received was not what they expected. The Secret Service stated that, even though staff working within Congress were stringently vetted, their political, religious or racial beliefs were subject to change at any time, and only continuous checking could identify the possibility of an internal assassin emerg-ing, and even then there was no guarantee that anything could be done to stop that person from inflicting harm.

Although some measures were taken to reduce the risk of weapons being brought into the chamber, including metal detectors, sophisti-cated x-ray machines and an increase in security guards, the Secret Ser-vice now sees the possibility of an internal assassin as the greatest threat to the President. In contrast, their worst nightmare was illustrated in the

Hollywood blockbuster movie *In the Line of Fire*, starring Clint Eastwood, when an assassin smuggled a home-made wooden gun through tight security in an attempt to kill the President. The story line was taken from a book, but the film was enhanced with the help of the Secret Service itself, after movie directors called in the agency to ensure that the film was as realistic as possible. 'Thankfully,' said one Secret Service bodyguard, 'no such weapon exists. But if it did!'

Bodyguards did not become a permanent feature of political life in Britain until after the killing of Lord Cavendish, the Irish Secretary of State, and Thomas Burke, Under Secretary to Dublin, in 1882. Both were mutilated by a crazed gang armed with knives. These new 'guardians' were not true bodyguards in the sense of the word. Mainly drawn from senior police ranks and issued with firearms, their primary role was to guard key points around the country. Few, if any, were deployed to provide personal protection, as many senior politicians within the cabinet saw the offer of bodyguards as 'ungentlemanly'.

Even the assassination of Spencer Perceval by John Bellingham (who was tried and hanged in the same week), and later the Suffragette movement, which often breached lazy security to cause violent assaults on may MPs, including Liberal Prime Minister Herbert Asquith, his Home Secretary, Winston Churchill, and Asquith's successor, David Lloyd George, did little to change political protection.

It was only after Lloyd George was hit for the third time by a Suffragette that things improved, but only slightly, and to some extent the poorly trained bodyguards actually made matters worse. Many showed a callous and merciless disregard to any female who came within arm's reach, and soon the campaign turned into a battle of the sexes.

Political reliance on personal protection was controlled more by public image than by the need to stay alive, and even during times of war British Prime Ministers considered their personal security unimportant. The most notable of these was Winston Churchill, who, even during the most turbulent times, employed only one trusted Scotland Yard bodyguard, Detective Inspector W. H. Thompson. Like many of his modern-day successors, Churchill detested the thought of increased security and refused to be hampered by bodyguards like his counterparts, Stalin and Roosevelt. If Churchill was lax about his security, his enemy, the Italian dictator Benito Mussolini, was not. But the more unpopular the leader, the more bodyguards he required, and Mussolini had reasons to be paranoid, having survived six assassination attempts. Mussolini employed over 300 personal bodyguards and used a variety of tactics to ward off assassination, even riding as a motorcycle outrider in one of his own motorcades. Yet despite these precautions nothing could save him as the Allied armies marched closer to his front door, and his reign was ended with a rope and a lamppost on a cold wet morning. It would be another four decades before British politicians would deem it necessary to use the same saturation of protection, and for totally different reasons.

Since Scotland Yard began supplying bodyguards to protect politicians, around the end of the last century, they have achieved a remarkable record in keeping themselves and their charges alive. The first, and last, Special Branch bodyguard to die on duty was Detective Sergeant Den Maclaughlan. The young and faithful guardian of Lord Kitchener died at the side of his charge when the warship HMS *Hampshire* struck a mine and plunged to the bottom of the icy sea. Rescued sailors later reported seeing Maclaughlan standing obediently behind Lord Kitchener on the starboard side of the quarterdeck. To many it seemed strange that he appeared not to be making any attempt to get Kitchener to the lifeboats, but one Branch bodyguard said solemnly: 'When you know your time has come, you just have to accept it and bite the bullet.'

Few Branch bodyguards have had to 'bite the bullet' in the last two decades, mainly because of the improvement in training, but also because VIPs now heed their guardians' advice. The world has seen over 800 VIP assassinations since the Second World War, including twelve presidents, three prime ministers and six other national leaders. Mahatma Gandhi opened the score, and the most recent victim was Yitzhak Rabin, Prime Minister of Israel.

Most of the world's national leaders have joined that élite club of survivors of an assassination attempt, including Richard Nixon, Ronald Reagan, Margaret Thatcher and Mikhail Gorbachev. Yet at the other end of the scale countless numbers of junior ministers, who often regarded their security in an almost dilettante way, paid the price with their lives. Many might say that those who choose a career in politics must be prepared to accept the risks it brings, for they knowingly step into the political arena and enjoy the attention they receive, unlike members of the Royal Family, who are born in the glare of the media and cannot simply walk away.

Politicians, on the other hand, argue that because they have influence beyond the grasp of the ordinary citizen they instantly become the target of the professional assassin. Their need for the professional bodyguard, which escalates as they climb the promotion ladder, is only to ensure they can carry out their duties in the best interest of the public. Whichever side one takes, it is unquestionably true that high-profile leaders are more at risk then the rest of the populace, and as that risk has grown so has the number of personal protection officers employed to shoulder the burden of responsibility, though only so far as their principal will allow.

Although to outsiders little would appear to have changed in the world of close protection, the transition has been wide-ranging and significant. Not only does the Prime Minister now switch cars in a remote corner of a motorway lay-by while on the way to his family home near Huntingdon, but he also has an entourage of protection officers working in advance of an impending visit, which could be to Bradford or Paris, to keep his personal protection team informed of any developments. However, with each new administration comes new perceptions and attitudes toward security.

Although Lady Thatcher remains under a heavy blanket of security more than seven years after leaving office, her successor, John Major, has never been prepared to hide from the threat of Irish terrorism, nor be blackmailed into taking an aggressive stance on protection. Only hours after his success in the party election for a new leader he 'toned down' recommendations to improve ministerial security. Out went the recommendation to wear a bulletproof vest, the weekly 'debugging' sweeps of his private office and quarters, and the recommendation to reduce his accessibility to the people, evident in the subsequent general election, when he refused to cut the number of public appearances in favour of the more restrictive but safer television interview. This decision concerned his bodyguards, not least because of the government's unpopularity at the time. Although the Prime Minister was pelted with eggs and heckled by a minority in the crowd, he continued his exhaustive 'soap-box' tour around the UK and easily won the people's vote, much to the delight of his party but to the disdain of his apprehensive protection team, who had, in their words, 'reputations to maintain and jobs to lose'.

There are certain security procedures in force over which even the Prime Minister has no control, including the restriction of information to key journalists and the procurement of security devices to keep pace with technological advancement. The Prime Minister is also obliged to listen, patiently, to his security advisers, but whether he heeds that advice can only be surmised. Some sights remain unchanged, including the familiar convoy of armoured Rovers parked outside 10 Downing Street, silhouetted against the anti-bomb-blast windows protected by the traditional famous black wrought-iron railings that provide the symbolic policeman with a leaning post during the long, boring night hours.

Even the most harmless of public occasions can turn into a tragic political disaster if allowed to do so, and this threat must always be taken seriously by government protection agencies. Stopping such a tragedy calls for a heavy blanket of security around world leaders. For Britain's Prime Minister this blanket includes a 30-man security team working, theoretically, three shifts in 24 hours, not including the government's Car Service Chauffeur or, as ministers prefer to call him, 'the driver'. On the other side of the Atlantic the US President maintains three eighteen-man protection teams with an additional team on standby, or, if demand requires it, working as a 'covert' defensive screen. These teams are supplemented by motorcycle outriders and local uniformed police officers. Within the UK these outriders are provided by the Metropolitan Police's Special Escort Group under the umbrella of SO14's Royalty Protection Branch, and in the USA the local police force outriders are controlled directly by the Secret Service.

Not all members of a government administration would have access to such a high profile of mobile security. In fact, within Britain only the Royal Family, the Prime Minister, and visiting heads of state or government are entitled to it, while in the USA the beneficiaries are the President, Vice-President and visiting heads of state.

Personal protection, on the other hand, has much wider coverage. While the Royal Family insist on minimum protection, the Prime Minister, Deputy Prime Minister, Chancellor of the Exchequer and Secretary of State for Foreign and Commonwealth Affairs are covered by a full 24-hour detail of personal protection, including travel security. The remaining members of the cabinet make do with a 'driver' if they are lucky, or public transport if not.

If the Prime Minister travels by train, a compartment will be reserved and the stationmaster will be there to see him off and at the other end another will meet him. When journeys further afield are necessary, an aircraft from the Queen's Flight will be made available and the Prime Minister is saluted off the ground by a senior RAF officer. On-board secure communications are provided, with direct links to Downing Street and Whitehall.

In the USA only the President and Vice-President receive full Secret Service protective cover, except during presidential elections, when all nominees are offered agency cover. The Secret Service also covers key US officials on overseas duties, but this is rare. Other mortals, such as the Chief of the Defence Staff, are provided with a small contingent of military bodyguards, supplemented by a chauffeur.

Presidential protection is a complex web that requires an assortment of government agencies, providing either the preventive or curative response. Both fanatics and terrorists regard the US President as a highly prized target, especially taking into account that his main responsibilities are 'to manage the nation's affairs' while, more importantly, providing a 'symbol to unify and hold the country together'. Killing the President would shatter this unifying factor and undermine public trust and morale. The killing of Kennedy proves this, particularly when, over 30 years later, the country is still divided over the truth, more having been written on this one subject then any other in modern American history.

The worldwide effect that the assassination of the President would have cannot be overstated. At worse, putting to one side the nation's reaction, his killing would immediately sow the seeds of doubt within many Third World developing countries. Future capital investment and share prices on the world's largest stock exchanges would undoubtedly slump as corporate clients sold in preparation for the uncertainty a new administration would bring. The result would be the loss of millions of dollars in revenue, leading to a rise in interest rates to compensate for the increase in bad debt, quickly followed by the collapse of the exchange rates and, ultimately, a global recession equal to, or worse than, that of the early 1990s.

It is therefore not surprising that the man whose murder would have such a detrimental effect on the world's economy has the tightest security screen on the planet. For the men and women of the Secret Service who shoulder the burden of this ring of steel, the responsibility is enormous. Preparation for presidential protection begins months in advance of his election to power, when a small four-men team of senior advisers is dispatched to each of the challengers' camps to begin building the protective fence. They also 'educate' the presidential candidate. As the race hots up and candidates are eliminated, so does their Secret Service protection, but only to strengthen other candidates' protection or the White House screen. This came about as a direct response to the Robert Kennedy assassination. Although the challenger still has considerably more freedom than the campaigning President, his daily lifestyle changes in every respect; rarely will he be left alone. Many of his public visits will be vetted, rearranged and sometimes cancelled, often to his displeasure. Although the Secret Service is quick to point out that he is unlikely to win votes as a dead challenger, it rarely fails to win the argument.

As the newly elected President bathes in the universal congratulations and his bitterest opponents become enthusiastic supporters, his entourage of aides discreetly increases. Secret Service agents tactfully move to fill the holes within his security screen and Army Signals Corps Officers fall in at the rear, often carrying the ominous black briefcases with 'FOR THE PRESIDENT'S EYES ONLY' embossed in gold across the rim. The presence of senior military commanders is the only outward sign of the briefcases' deadly content; the nuclear security codes that enable the President to initiate Armageddon.

Within hours, Congress is eager to approve the President's nominations and pass his bills. Foreign ambassadors scurry to arrange meetings, while global heads of state and government hasten to attract one of his few overseas visits. But first the President must be briefed by his personal protection team. It is a fallacy that Secret Service agents are the only people able to tell the President what to do. Admittedly they can sway his opinion and deter him from a particular course of action. It also goes without saying that if ordered 'Get down, Mr President', he will instantly obey. Nevertheless, the final decision is his and his alone, as it always has been. Whether he listens to that 'advice' can be largely determined by his background and personality. John F. Kennedy loved to meet the people, and up to his death many of his predecessors had been accessible to the American public. Even for a short time after there was little change to this. Kennedy's successor, Lyndon Johnson, often broke all the Secret Service 'security rules' to shake the hands of his people, even to the point where they would rip at his flesh, causing deep cuts that needed treatment from his doctor. But Johnson loved impulsive crowd behaviour and appeared to feel no pain; in fact he would often describe each cut to his aides with great pleasure and affection.

Presidents Nixon, Carter and Bush also enjoyed contact with the people, showing deep emotional awareness of the importance of physical contact and stating that every hand shaken was another guaranteed election vote. Secret Service agents often joked privately that during Carter's administration his only policy of office was to shake the hand of every US citizen. Some other holders of office have not been so inclined. Ford, Reagan, and more recently Bill Clinton, have all been happy to conduct their presidencies with little or no public contact. Yet both categories of President have been the target of assassination, the most famous being the killing of Kennedy, equalled two decades later by the wounding of Ronald Reagan in 1981, proving that even limited public access does not deter the assassin, whether professional or irrational.

Eight Presidents have found themselves in the line of fire since the first attempted presidential assassination, on Andrew Jackson in 1835. But few world leaders today would take the same action as Jackson, who battered his assailant unconscious with a walking stick.

However, all of these attempted assassinations, successful or not, had one distinct feature in common; the assassins (or supposed assassins) had given some kind of advance warning before they struck.

Sally Moore, who attempted to shoot Gerald Ford in 1975, had telephoned the Secret Service, FBI and San Francisco police and given a warning, albeit incoherently, only hours before she opened fire, missing Ford by five feet and hitting a wall. Three years before, Arthur Bremer had stalked Nixon during his 1972 presidential election and given countless warnings to the FBI of his intention to kill the President. These were passed to the Secret Service, which tightened security and unknowingly deflected the attack toward another presidential candidate, Governor George Wallace of Alabama, who, without the protective resources of the President, was shot and paralysed. More recently, Bill Clinton has also faced those determined to inflict harm, in particular the Maryland man who crashed a light aeroplane into the south-facing wall of the White House and the Colorado man who fired 29 shots at the north-facing wall of the mansion. Both men were said to be suffering from depression and had no intention of killing the President, but the intense media coverage created by these two incidents led to other, more damaging breaches in security at the White House.

The nocturnal drive-past shooting was followed soon after by the Oklahoma bombing, which forced Secret Service bodyguards to recommend the closure of Pennsylvania Avenue to prevent a similar car or lorry bomb. Only days later Secret Service agent Scott Giambattista was shot and wounded by a fellow agent as he tackled Leland Modjeski, a 37-year-old male from Washington's Virginia suburbs armed with a pistol, who had climbed the wrought-iron fence surrounding the south lawn and had managed to get within 30 yards of the mansion. It was the first time Secret Service agents had had to draw their weapons since the shooting of Reagan in 1981. Coincidentally, it was also the first time an agent had been wounded in the line of duty since Special Agent Tim McCarthy took a bullet in the abdomen to protect Reagan. While Giambattista was attended immediately by paramedics, McCarthy had to wait in agony for seventeen minutes. In the words of one bodyguard at the time, 'He was the least of our problems.'

Soon after the shooting incident, police shot dead a homeless man as he ran across Pennsylvania Avenue toward the White House, brandishing a knife, but what threat he posed to the President was debatable. The last time a White House intruder was killed was in 1976, when it was claimed that incompetent security compounded by trigger-happy officers had caused an unnecessary death. However, Bill Clinton shrugged off recent incidents with the quip, 'just another day at the White House'.

Breaches of the ten-foot-high fence surrounding the world's most famous building are not uncommon. During 1989-94 it was scaled 23 times, and in the five years preceding 1989 it was breached twice as often. Although no official White House records are kept, the local police department averages one call-out per night directly related to infringements of the security fence. Even if they had the massive resources needed, Secret Service agents could not prevent these violations, quite simply because the White House is America's biggest tourist attraction, and cannot be seen as an impenetrable fortress within what is, essentially, an open society.

At about the same time, similar 'attempts' directed at the British Prime Minister were publicised within Britain, although these, too, were highly debatable 'threats', the first being more of a farce than any real threat to life. A youth, Robert Gipters, fired three shots from a starting pistol as the Prime Minister's motorcade drove into his secluded country home near Huntingdon, Cambridgeshire. The youth was pounced on by armed police officers and arrested. He later told detectives he was suffering from depression and was oblivious to the fact that the limousine contained a VIP. Special Branch bodyguards protecting the Prime Minister were totally unaware of the incident until some hours later, when journalists questioned the leader about his apparently lax security. His reply, 'I have full confidence in my security team' failed to hide the confused expressions he and his team showed. Only later did it emerge that the local police chief had failed to brief the Prime Minister's bodyguards about the incident. Nevertheless, even if he had been informed, the leader would still not have heard the shots, because all armoured limousines are not only bulletproof but soundproof, something Lyndon Johnson had noticed soon after taking delivery of a new armoured limousine. The problem was rectified by installing an electronic gadget to relay external crowd noise inside the tank-like shell.

The second incident affecting Britain's Prime Minister was not so much an attempt as a future possibility, and even now the intended victim is not known. The story began in early 1995, when forestry workers uncovered a concrete prison cell concealed underground and deep within undergrowth in Thetford forest. Detailed maps with drawings pinpointing the Prime Minister's country home and the Queen's Sandringham estate were also found. Police sounded a massive security alert and, after weeks of covert surveillance by a specially trained team of officers, a man was seen leaving the bunker and was followed to a flat in Norwich. Scotland Yard's anti-terrorist branch were not convinced that the structure was a prison cell. They believed it was an old empty IRA ammunition store, similar to those found within remote regions of 'bandit country' in Armagh, Northern Ireland, and requested the continuance of undercover surveillance. However, owing to local police resentment of this apparent outside interference, the man was arrested before the order could be confirmed.

It is still not known how the structure came to be built unnoticed. One senior officer working on the case at the time told the author: 'It's quite a sophisticated job and far too large to be constructed by one man.' He added: 'The Prime Minister abduction theory just does not add up when taking into account his tight security; only a madman would attempt it ... but whoever, or whatever, was destined for the underground bunker we will never know.' Detectives later released a man on bail and ordered the bunker destroyed.

Although such incidents are rare, they show that activists are still preparing for that one opportunity to exploit relaxed security. The foregoing incident also highlights how the breakdown of communications and lack of co-operation between police forces can seriously undermine the protection bodyguards provide, no matter how well trained or experienced they may be.

Improvements in security around the White House have not stopped at closing Pennsylvania Avenue. There has been a noticeable increase in security guards, who are as vigilant as they are pleasant.

The erection of concrete barriers around the mansion complements the sophisticated access-control computers situated at the gatehouse, which is manned by the additional security officers. It is understandable that, with the current President receiving more death threats than any of his predecessors, his customary jog along the mall has been stopped and he makes use of a running machine within the mansion or jogs at a nearby military base surrounded by tight security.

The President is considered at his safest inside the grounds of the White House. Visitors are vetted weeks in advance by Secret Service agents, and guests invited to formal ceremonies are carefully scrutinised and checked against government security files. Visitors inside the building are restricted in their movements and controlled by electronic 'tagging'. Each 'tag' issued gives off a microwave code that automatically opens doors when they are approached, and those not authorised to enter certain areas will be refused access and the control room alerted.

Even if Clinton has made the White House a place that 'buzzes with the energy, exuberance and informality of a college campus', parts of the White House, such as the Oval Office and adjoining rooms, are restricted to only the most senior members of the administration and guarded by Secret Service agents backed up by closed-circuit television and panic alarms. Visitors given access to these 'red' areas are always accompanied either by a Secret Service agent or the person they are visiting. The President, while within this impenetrable defence, is not normally accompanied by a personal bodyguard, although one will surely be within shouting distance.

Visiting journalists rarely see the in-depth security measures in place, mainly because many of the official or presidential briefings are given outside on the White House lawn or in a separate conference room with no direct access to the 'red' areas. Although the Secret Service would prefer to keep the President under the safety of the White House security umbrella and away from the public's physical contact, he will inevitably be compelled to undertake many official visits as part of his duties. When this is necessary, it is the Secret Service's intention to make the security arrangements of the White House portable, with the ability to surround the President whenever he ventures outside the grounds and replace the mansion's walls with Secret Service agents acting as human shields.

While the President does not have the powers of a monarch, he is treated like one in both his public and private life. White House bodyguards are there to ensure the President's safety, but also to see that the rules of etiquette are not broken. The President's body should never be touched except as a formal greeting when shaking hands, and he is never to be jostled in crowds or slapped on the back by the public, as happened to Nixon in early 1970, resulting in serious bruising.

Over the years a series of 'security rules' have come into play which effectively defend against such improper actions. Secret Service bodyguards now insist that all official trips are concluded as fast as possible and with the avoidance of crowds. If this is not possible, the crowds should be gathered where they can be controlled and watched, and, to ensure this, every high vantage point is commandeered for anti-sniping teams. Crowds should never be positioned closer than 30 feet, and Secret Service bodyguards use a secondary close protection team, in addition to the local police, to block or immobilise any over-zealous party intent on touching the President.

These precautions are effective only until the President decides to meet the crowd, a decision over which the Secret Service has no control, but one for which they have now adopted procedures to ensure his protection. The moment the President moves off the designated path (of which he would have been briefed before the visit) and toward the gathered crowd, bodyguards providing a close-protection screen leave their positions and discreetly form a physical barrier between the President and the gathered crowd, maintaining constant eye contact with covert watchers mingling with the spectators.

During Mikhail Gorbachev's visit to London in 1989 no such precautions were adopted by his personal protection team. This left him vulnerable to attack and caused much apprehension within British bodyguard circles, whose help and advice had been refused. This was unusual, as political protection is normally easier abroad, and none more so than presidential protection. Host nations are more than happy to fulfil any requests made to them by the Secret Service; the last thing any government needs is the death of a President on its soil, for undoubtedly the blame will be left embarrassingly on its doorstep.

Some weeks before the visit, a group of representatives from the protection team will arrive to familiarise themselves with each venue to be visited, and also to establish the ground rules regarding who is responsible for what. During President Clinton's visit to London late in 1995, Secret Service agents arrived in May to observe the Hyde Park VE Day celebrations secretly. There were more VIPs gathered for this occasion than for any other event this century, including 18 heads of state, 36 heads of government and 123 ambassadors and diplomats. They were accompanied by more than 500 personal bodyguards, not including the extra Special Branch protection teams and SAS bodyguards drafted in for the occasion. To say the US Secret Service was impressed by the tight security and smoothness of the event would be an understatement. In meetings with Special Branch officers and SAS commanders, Secret Service agents made few, if any requests beyond the normal criteria that personal protection and mobile security should be provided by White House bodyguards, and they were happy to leave close and covert protection in the hands of Scotland Yard.

The only problem to arise concerned the authorisation of the carrying and use of smoke and CS gas canisters, which, the Secret Service assured, would only be used to cover a withdrawal in the event of an attack. British security commanders were reluctant to approve such a request, although they did provide firearms licences for the use of automatic sub-machine guns and pump-action shotguns, knowing of the lethal consequences if they were used in a London street. Another area that caused much debate concerned who would drive the presidential limousine. Secret Service agents were reluctant to repeat the same embarrassing farce that had dogged President Carter's visit to Britain in 1985, when supposed specially trained drivers ware unable to control the heavy steering amid the phalanx of White House bodyguards surrounding the vehicle on foot as it drove through the unaccommodating streets of Durham. A compromise was reached when it was agreed that two government chauffeurs would travel to the USA to be trained by the Secret Service in how to drive the armoured Cadillac, which weighs in excess of five tons and has a maximum speed of 40mph.

The Clinton visit also saw the use of the 'double bluff' tactic. For example, two airports, Heathrow and Stanstead, were ordered to make identical preparations for the President's arrival. Only at the last minute was it decided that Air Force One would land at Heathrow, much to the displeasure of those waiting at Stanstead. The double bluff is not a new tactic. It was used during the Gorbachev visit in 1987 and proved popular with bodyguards, the airports alerted in that case being RAF Brize Norton and RAF Lyneham in Wiltshire. Also on that occasion, as on the Clinton visit, two venues were picked for every occasion but only one used. When the President was ready to fly out from Heathrow at the end of his trip, the media showed his motorcade driving through the streets of London toward Heathrow, but the President was overhead in a helicopter borrowed from the Queen's Flight.

Another facet of presidential or prime ministerial protection about which little is known concerns air travel by VIPs. Commonsense may dictate that protection is provided by the VIP's air force or the air force of the host nation. However, the confusion begins when the VIP is flying in international airspace or over unfriendly territory, which happened during Gorbachev's visit to the West in 1989. His aircraft had to pass through Russian, German, French and British airspace. At that time there was little trust between Gorbachev's protection team (predominantly from the KGB) and the Western air forces. Western governments refused to allow 'war-ready' Soviet fighter escorts to fly over their territory for obvious reasons, and similarly the Russian leader's bodyguards refused the offer of Western fighter escorts. There was, and still is, no simple answer for dealing with two opposing heads of state when in the air, even when they agree to meet on 'neutral ground'. Often it is out of the protection team's domain, and the matter is left in the expert hands of the diplomats.

Presidential protection has two sides; the one we know so well of alert, unsmiling bodyguards surrounding the President, and the other of men hiding in the shadows, unseen or unheard of until events such as those centred on President Bush's visit to Panama in 1991.

The trip had been planned some months before and prior notice had not been given. However, as soon as the President landed the word quickly spread and a minority prepared an anti-government demonstration. As the group marched on the outdoor rally at which Bush was guest of honour, local police officers, in an attempt to disperse the crowd and minimise embarrassment, opened fire with tear gas and water cannon. Two hundred yards away and out of sight, Secret Service bodyguards standing close to the President heard the pops of tear gas canisters and, believing it to be sniper fire, immediately moved to protect 'the eagle', as the Service calls him. Within seconds the President and his wife were draped in bulletproof trenchcoats and escorted to the safety of a nearby trailer. Simultaneously, and for the first time in public, black-clad figures from the Counter-Assault Team, complete with gasmasks and M16 assault rifles, erupted from behind the President and stormed into a nearby office block which bodyguards had identified as containing the sniper.

The team were members of the military's Special Operations Group, Delta Force, working on secondment from the regiment for periods of up to six months, or whenever required by the Secret Service. Presidential visits abroad are a more complicated issue for the Counter-Assault Team, for, with few countries prepared to allow the unit access, a compromise normally has to be reached. In the case of President Clinton's visit to Britain in 1995, the Counter-Assault Team was provided by members of the counter-revolutionary warfare wing of the SAS, who, conforming to regulations, provided the Prime Minister with similar protective cover. Even in a motorcade formation the assault team will be carefully appended to the rear, concealed within a van with blacked-out windows.

Yet the Secret Service continues to deny the existence of such units, even though the Panama incident was witnessed, and recorded, by the NBC news network and American photo-journalists. In fact the denial can go much further. During private conversations between the author and Secret Service bodyguards, the unit's existence was again refuted, albeit behind a wry smile.

The integration of this type of unit into the spectrum of political protection, to support rather than dominate, is just another step along the road toward both a pro-active and reactive response to assassination. Yet it is also the first sign that the military, within countries where bodyguarding is ostentatiously a police force's task, are playing a much more important role than ever before. It is also an indication of mounting concern over VIP protection. Whereas attitudes regarding staying alive were previously filled with rhetoric and false promises, today political protection is enhanced in secret and without public approval.

The cost of such protective measures is rarely justified or even explained by government administrators. Over the last three decades the financial burden of keeping VIPs alive has soared far beyond anyone's comprehension. Maintaining the Secret Service in 1968 cost a mere $17.6 million, whereas today the cost is closer to $47.5 million. These enormous costs are due to the often elaborate security measures implemented in protecting the President and his wife and children. This alone can drain in excess of $13 million dollars a year. There are also the ex-Presidents to consider. Carter, Ford, Reagan and Bush all receive full Secret Service protection, and currently the agency has half of its manpower on 'overseas assignments', protecting diplomats and US representatives in the former Yugoslavia, the Middle East and Russia. Although the British and Australian agencies are not as large, the cost is just as high.

The fact that the US President and his wife are the most heavily guarded couple on earth could not have escaped even the most casual onlookers. This is unlikely to change in the foreseeable future. However, with many nations attempting to forge ahead with peace, and American diplomats playing a key part in the secret negotiations, it is reasonable to assume that diplomats and peace envoys will be challenging for that top spot in the future.

5

Diplomacy or Death

Diplomats are a privileged caste who live outside the normal rules of law governing the country to which they are sent. Treaties dating back centuries bar diplomatic representatives from both civil and criminal laws. They cannot be fined for speeding or illegal parking, and their embassies, missions and residences are out of bounds to provincial police forces, even if the authorities know a crime has been committed or a terrorist is being shielded. However, such privileges come at a price. Diplomacy remains one of the most dangerous occupations in the world. The mortality and kidnap statistics easily exceed those of any other profession, and make gangster assassinations look meagre by comparison.

Between 1963 and 1995 approximately 750 diplomatic representatives of 112 countries were murdered; of these 185 were assassinated, which does not include the 25 representatives slaughtered during civil strife in Africa and Latin America. Worse is the record of embassy staff injured and maimed at the hands of fanatical terrorist groups, often while working abroad. One notable case was the suicide bomb attack on the US Embassy in Beirut during April 1983, in which 61 people were killed, including the CIA station chief, Charles Ames, and nine of his special agents, three of whom were acting as bodyguards. During this same period a further 43 diplomats were kidnapped or held prisoner while on official business, and two were never seen again.

Host governments have a duty to protect the lives and property of diplomats visiting or resident within their country. This basic requirement is over 300 years old and dates back to the forerunners of diplomats, who were no more than messengers of truce or, as was more often the case, bearers of a declaration of war. But even then it was in both parties' interests to allow the messenger to return unhindered and alive. The old saying 'Don't shoot the messenger' was used just as much then as it is today, though its meaning was far more serious. However, today terrorist organisations are not prepared to adhere to ancient customs and traditions which over the centuries have become internationally accepted regulations supported by international laws.

Historically, diplomats have two main functions; to act as spokespersons for their sovereigns, and to communicate the reception they received. The formal recognition of diplomacy as a respected profession had to wait until the Congress of Vienna in 1815, but it was not until 1893 that ambassadors were to become a worldwide phenomenon used effectively by governments to convey messages of support or disharmony.

One of the first masters of the practice of diplomacy was the Papacy, and Pope Pius II had himself been an envoy to numerous courts between 1435 and 1438, including that of Scotland's King James I. Over time the Vatican established a network of delegates whose job it was to keep the Vatican informed of political and religious developments throughout Christendom. Even today the church maintains diplomatic links with many of the world's governments, and requests for it to act as an intermediary during delicate negotiations are not uncommon. The US withdrawal from Vietnam came after much Vatican intervention, and delegates acting under the Pope's personal instructions have recently been involved in peace negotiations in Bosnia and the Middle East.

There are numerous regulations protecting diplomats, including the Vienna Convention on Diplomatic and Consular Relations, the Convention on the Privileges and Immunities of the United Nations, and the Convention on the Prevention and the Punishment of Crimes against Internationally Protected Persons including diplomatic agents. However, representatives still have to rely on the nation's police force for their physical protection unless they are on a mission of international importance or of high risk, when a team of military bodyguards would be provided. Police protection is all very well in Western cities such as London or Washington, where the police have a great deal of respect and maintain an excellent reputation, but elsewhere, such as Latin America and Africa, standards vary enormously from the terrible to the non-existent. Even some Western police forces are restricted in the protection they can provide, mainly owing to the size of the diplomatic community. London, for example, has over 135 ambassadors and 5,000 diplomats, all located in 460 buildings, and that excludes the 20,000 family members. One senior police officer said: 'It would take the entire manpower of the Metropolitan Police to cover all these potential targets within that small area, and given our resources and increasing commitments it would be impossible to do.'

Most embassies in London are provided with a uniformed armed police officer from Scotland Yard's Diplomatic Protection Branch (SO16), supported by an armed back-up only two minutes away, the fastest response time in the country. Others prefer to employ their own 24-hour protection, like the American and Israeli embassies, which either fly over 'ex-military' bodyguards or employ a British private security company using ex-special forces personnel. Embassies are also given regular security inspections by a team of police and military experts which usually includes an officer from the SAS counter-revolutionary warfare team, who offers recommendations for improvements. Yet many ambassadors resent these 'oppressive and restrictive recommendations' and refuse to install cameras, locked doors, security passes and extra armed guards, arguing that it goes against the fabric of consular relations with the public. Ambassadors also plead that they have to promote their country as a safe place to visit in order to attract tourist and business travel. Locking themselves behind armour plated glass and Star Trek-style sliding doors goes against this image of freedom and openness.

Police security advisers have no powers to force embassies to improve their security. They can only advise or strongly recommend, in the hope that their words are heeded, although unfortunately they seldom are. Security teams feel they are fighting a losing battle against officialdom because embassies, particularly in London, normally occupy the oldest and most prestigious buildings, which are nearly always listed for their architectural significance and protected by heritage laws, preventing their alteration to meet the needs of today's security conscious world. But while the government is prepared to protect historic buildings for future generations, terrorists are not, and the deliberate targeting of such buildings to create greater media interest has been commonplace. The Provisional IRA proved this in 1991 when they detonated a massive lorry bomb outside a 600-year-old church in the heart of the financial capital of London, reducing the grade three listed building to rubble.

The personal protection of ambassadors and diplomats living within the United Kingdom was another controversial issue until 1975. Britain was one of the few countries which still refused to allow representatives to use their own protection teams, with the exception of the American and Israeli ambassadors, who were considered to be at unusually high risk. But as a compromise some selected ambassadors were offered a two-man protection team from Scotland Yard's A squad, although the offer was normally rejected because, as we have seen elsewhere, they were not the most efficient of bodyguards at that time. The attempted abduction of Princess Anne in 1974 did little to improve their reputation.

Diplomats were soon to become the most popular of all terrorist targets, mainly owing to their high status but also because of their lax security. The days when the diplomat was beyond the threat of murder were gone. The kidnapping of Charles Elbrick, the US Ambassador to Brazil, in September 1969 was the first of a reported 21 such incidents involving diplomats up to 1971. Many experts now agree that, in retrospect, this figure would have been vastly reduced but for the authorities' constant acceptance of the kidnappers' demands, often for money and the release of political prisoners. Despite these concessions, not all of the victims were lucky enough to live. Count von Spreti, the German Ambassador to Guatemala, was abducted and brutally slaughtered early in 1970, and a decade later secret negotiations between a group of Colombian terrorists and a British private security company ended in failure when it became apparent to the security company that the ambassadorial aide the group was holding was already dead.

To plug the gaps, British diplomats working in South America were provided with bodyguards from the Royal Military Police, whereas visiting VIPs and government ministers had the luxury of SAS protection. The first to receive such security, albeit at his own request, was Sir Anthony Royle, parliamentary under-secretary to the Foreign and Commonwealth Office, during a ministerial tour of the region. Royle's exclusive position within the Foreign Office allowed him to secure a foothold for the SAS in protecting senior members of the government while on overseas visits, a foothold that was to continue and expand throughout the 1970s and early 1980s. Soon after the first SAS bodyguard, Major Andrew Nightingale, was appointed Royle's guardian, further assignments and top-secret protection tasks were passed to the regiment, including the surveying of areas where over-seas diplomats were most at risk. For this delicate task a close colleague of Nightingale was used, Major David Walker. An experienced ex-Royal Engineer who had been one of the original members of the regiment's bodyguard advisory team and had instructed both the Turkish Head of State and the Shah of Iran on personal security, he was to advise British Embassies in Uruguay, Brazil, Argentina and Bolivia on improvements to their security.

Walker and Nightingale's involvement was not simply to give the regiment something to do, but a direct response to the kidnapping of the British Ambassador to Uruguay, Geoffrey Jackson, in 1970. Jackson was an intelligent diplomat who had realised he was being stalked many months before he was seized. The art of counter-surveillance was something he had learnt early in his career, and was matched only by his skill in diplomacy. However, when he reported back to the Foreign Office about his concerns they replied with benign indifference. Their misjudgment became evident when Jackson disappeared, and journalists were as merciless in reporting the gaffe as those holding the ambassador.

Although Jackson had a three-man military protection team he had prohibited them from carrying firearms, which resulted in their inability to do much when he was pistol whipped and dragged away by the heavily armed terrorists. Not surprisingly, Jackson relied upon the weapon of diplomacy to keep him and his bodyguards alive, a decision that was vindicated only after the corpses of bodyguards lay scattered in the streets of Europe on two separate occasions, after the abductions of Hans Martin Schleyer in Germany and Aldo Moro in Italy.

At about the same time assassination and abduction threats were made against Sir David Hunt, the British Ambassador in Rio. The department, determined not to fail again, requested additional body-guards from the Royal Military Police, and duly got them. In addition to this security, advisors from the SAS flew immediately to the embassy in Rio, not to supplement the personal protection team, as was reported in the British press, but to identify weaknesses within it.

Closer to home, diplomatic protection remained in the hands of the Special Branch so far as the mainland was concerned, although in Northern Ireland the Royal Military Police expanded its basic frame-work of overseas diplomatic protection to include high court judges and foreign representatives, even though the former had nothing to do with the immediate risk to life but was more about suppressing para-noia. It was only after the murder of two crown court judges that a real need became apparent.

As terrorism in the Province became more elusive but pre-dictable, bodyguards could easily float between several targets while appearing to provide the 24-hour cover. More recently the IRA cease-fire made the method of 'trickle posting' more popular with police and military protection teams. In simple terms it allowed bodyguards to provide cover when the VIP is at his most vulnerable, when mobile or entering and exiting buildings. By carefully planning VIP schedules and engagements, protection officers or soldiers can be used to cover a number of VIPs. Naturally this type of close cover is not suitable for all clients, and is only successful if the VIP 'plays the game', in the words of one military bodyguard. It is also unfeasible when protecting a person with a high threat level, but proves sufficient when protect-ing foreign diplomats from territories such as Norway and Denmark, which are at little risk from terrorism or the deranged psychopath.

Both of these countries, plus Austria and Portugal, are known to use this method of protection, yet some private security companies within America and Britain are not convinced of its safety or practi-cality when covering a multitude of VIPs. In the words of one body-guard: 'Even with the best planners in the world it only takes one minor hold-up or delay to leave another client exposed.'

As terrorist attacks on embassies continued, the Royal Military Police took over responsibility for the security of overseas embassies from the private security company KMS. Despite the fact that it was new to the industry, the company had obtained the contract from the Foreign and Commonwealth Office in 1975. On the surface it showed little experience of close-protection work, but all three company directors were known to the British government for their service in the SAS, and one was still a serving member of the regiment when he began to work for the company. They were Brigadier Mike Wingate-Grey, a veteran of the SAS campaign in Aden, Colonel Jim Johnson, a veteran of the Yemen civil war, and David Walker, who moved from the highly successful security company Control Risks, which also had Foreign Office links in Latin America. Andrew Nightingale, Royle's bodyguard in South America, joined the company two years later to replace the retired Mike Wingate-Grey.

Overall, KMS fulfilled its role in averting potential assassination attempts during its employment, particularly within African states, even if the killing of Christopher Ewart-Biggs, the British Ambassador to Dublin who was blown to bits by an IRA culvert bomb placed under the road in 1976, made things untenable. But Ireland, and Dublin in particular, was out of bounds to the company anyway, mainly due to the political consequences if it became public knowledge that ex-special forces personnel were working south of the border and, probably more importantly, to avoid causing offence to the Irish police. Yet after Ewart-Biggs's death the oversight was quickly rectified and government-sponsored bodyguards were deployed, but only after permission had been gained from the Irish police, who were only too happy to pass the responsibility to someone else.

The Foreign Office's swing towards military bodyguards rather than private protection was nothing to do with the companies. It was simply a case of financial restrictions imposed by the incoming government. The cost of hiring protection from KMS and, to some degree Control Risks (although Control Risks was not actively involved in the direct protection of VIPs, but was used more for security advice and consultation, leaving the bodyguarding to others), was around £20,000 plus expenses per man used.

Mrs Thatcher's argument, possibly justified, was why should the government pay ex-military soldiers to do a job that the military were already capable of doing free of charge? However, the decision to divert the resources thus saved into expanding and improving the Royal Military Police (RMP) close-protection team failed owing to a lack of suitable manpower within the Corps, a problem that persists today. What the government had failed to realise was that the threat to overseas diplomats was expanding faster than the military Corps; and although today the military police remain Britain's leading exponent of bodyguard protection, providing the majority, but not all, of the close-protection teams for diplomats, the government still has to employ additional bodyguards from private security companies during hypersensitive times.

The Gulf War of 1990–1 was such an occasion. When Iraq invaded Kuwait, British embassies in the region become targets of the anti-coalition faction. Ambassadors in the region, many of whom were attempting shuttle diplomacy to prevent a war, were under increasing threat of an assassin's bullet. The RMPs were already overcommitted and unable to muster the needed manpower at such short notice, forcing the Foreign Office to employ a private security company. They achieved what the military were unable to do, and within six hours 25 ex-military and Special Branch bodyguards (many of the former had only recently left diplomatic protection teams) were on flights to Riyadh and Amman. The cost: £47,000 plus expenses per man. It was these men whom the British tabloid press wrongly identified as being members of a top-secret SAS infiltration squad. Anybody with SAS knowledge would have known that the regiment would not have been used in Baghdad, quite simply because, with the Americans running the show, intelligence gathering in the Iraqi capital would remain the sole domain of the CIA. In the media's rush to get a scoop they caused an international scandal that required weeks of behind-the-scenes diplomacy by the men the team were deployed to protect.

The Foreign and Commonwealth Office also employ their own 'in-house' security consultants, many of whom are Senior Executive Officers with Special Branch experience. Yet they rarely take on personal protection duties, concentrating on the detection and neutralisation of electronic bugging devices, with some limited assignments to identify gaps in embassy security and suggest improvements.

American and Australian diplomats have always been under even more pressure than their counterparts in Britain, especially during the Vietnam War, and of all the embassies in the world those of the USA have been the most irresistible for terrorist groups. The symbolic importance of the American diplomat makes him more prone to assassination or its close cousin, abduction. No one knows this better than the US State Department's Bureau of Diplomatic Security. Its unsuccessful attempts to standardise protection for its embassies across the globe only resulted in low morale and increased confusion. This was because embassy security was expanded and put in the hands of three different factions; the host government, Marine Corps security guards and embassy staff. In the case of the host government, who were unable to assign their own protective resources, the job of outer perimeter security was contracted out to local private companies.

Doubts over the arrangements first came to light when one of these companies highlighted the problem vividly. After obtaining the contract to provide the external security for a US Embassy in the Gulf, it employed local manpower to fill its posts. Although many were highly trained, professional and, above all, motivated to their duty, embassy staff became bewildered by the number of personnel seemingly performing the same tasks. The manning of three separate identity card checkpoints was one instance quoted in an internal departmental enquiry released in late 1990. The bickering began after embassy staff refused to conform to the company's imposed rules, which led to a breakdown in relations. In view of this disharmony, much of which was no fault of the security company employed, the State Department asked the host nation to deploy its own resources as a short-term solution, but it refused. A viable solution has not been found, but relations between embassy staff and security personnel have improved.

Embassy security is one thing, but the personal protection of diplomats is another. Unlike the simple security procedures that can be employed around an embassy, the procurement of bodyguards is a complex political problem, often involving several government agencies. Firstly, security advisers from the State Department must undertake an in-depth threat assessment to see if personal protection is warranted. Secondly, it must be decided who should provide the protection; the Marine Guard, private security or, on rare occasions, the Secret Service. However, this option of blanket cover would require a higher threat assessment than that of the President, which is all but impossible.

At this juncture security advisers working for the US State Department hit their first snag. As part of the risk assessment for diplomats about to work overseas, they are required to visit the State Department's Regional Security Officer or Legal Attaches Officer (the FBI's local person) in the country to be visited. However, attempts to obtain information about potential threats are hampered by a 1975 Executive Order signed by President Ford, barring the CIA or FBI from infiltrating terrorist groups to obtain information. This has resulted in there being little or no information on possible assassins outside the USA. To find the missing pieces of the jigsaw puzzle, threat assessors have to wade through endless reams of data, and even then no information may come to light. It all takes time; time the diplomat does not have.

The killing or kidnapping of an American diplomat not only violates the principles of international immunity but also causes an immediate crisis for the White House. Terrorists deliberately target US representatives, knowing that the government's policy of no negotiation and no concessions helps display its weakness, inability or unwillingness to honour its commitment to protect its nationals. For this reason diplomats are rarely kidnapped for financial reward alone. Although a ransom will undoubtedly be part of the group's demands, it will always be accompanied by a demand for the release of fellow-terrorist prisoners, the reading of a pre-prepared statement, and safe passage to a designated country.

Despite public statements to the contrary, governments do talk to terrorists, but there is a subtle difference between 'talk to' and 'negotiate with'. The former offers nothing and receives nothing in return, whereas the latter gives something in exchange for something. Governments never negotiate directly, but bring in 'intermediaries' to do it for them. These will often be other highly skilled foreign diplomats or individuals connected to the Vatican. The abduction of diplomats is a federal offence and puts political issues at stake, so under US law the highest level of government becomes involved. The President will speak to his closest advisors in his administration and in the military. Usually the knee-jerk reaction is to deploy extra bodyguards to the region, followed by dialogue with friendly nations to arrange intermediaries and to collate information on the abductors.

Although much of the grassroots intelligence would come from bodyguards working in the area, intelligence is only useful if taken seriously by those in Washington. For example, as the Beirut hostage crisis deepened in the middle of 1987, US special forces were ordered to plan a rescue. British and American bodyguards working in the country warned that the hostages were located in several buildings and moved frequently, but the intelligence was discounted by military commanders who favoured more 'in-touch' sources. It transpired after the Desert One debrief that these sources were at least four hours behind real-time movements, yet protection teams did not fare much better, being two hours behind, proving that even bodyguards are not infallible.

Occasionally the risk to an embassy or its staff becomes so great that not even the best protection available can prevent a terrorist attack. In such cases the only practical solution left to the White House administration is to close the embassy down and bring the staff home. Not surprisingly, the Middle East, closely followed by Latin America, has provided the greatest risks. Car or lorry bombs delivered by suicide fanatics is one such threat, the only deterrent being the erection of a secure compound with reinforced walls able to resist high-explosive blasts, where vehicles can be searched. This option was not favoured by the General Accounting Office but it was implemented anyway, only for the two embassies concerned, Beirut and Taiwan, to close soon after.

Diplomatic protection has been drastically upgraded since 1991, at an estimated cost of $6.4 billion and rising. Many bodyguards are sceptical of the American hardware solution, arguing that the bill for improving personal protection standards could be halved by ensuring that the right calibre of individual was selected and trained in the first place. As one British Foreign Office security advisor explained to the author: 'Buying advanced detection facilities, and installing high-tech TV surveillance equipment is all very well ... but it can only be used as an aid, not a cure. There is no substitute for the highly motivated, dedicated and switched-on employee.'

Embassy security in the former Soviet Union is another area requiring a different approach by today's bodyguards. The end of the Cold War may have brought a feeling of safety and security to the hearts of millions living within the frontiers of central Europe, but personal protection for diplomats in Moscow has proliferated to such a degree that it makes the American bodyguard boom of the 1960s look meagre by comparison. However, the threat does not come from politically orientated terrorists but from ruthless Mafia and underworld gangsters, intent on profiting from the billions of dollars in aid that poured into the country after the collapse of Communism. Extortion and racketeering are so widespread in central Moscow that no business is unaffected, and kidnapping is as common as queuing for milk. So far, no diplomatic staff have suffered such a fate, doubtless due to the sheer number of private and governmental bodyguards deployed. However, as one ambassador says, 'It's only a matter of time.' This rather sceptical view may have something to do with the escalation of incidents directed at embassy buildings. During 1992-4 there were four bomb attacks (albeit small ones) aimed at Western embassies, and at least three times that number of drive-by shootings.

Whereas Western security advisers were once paranoid about keeping secrets in and the former KGB out, a highly placed source now says: 'Today the KGB help keep the information in and the gangsters out. We've come a long way.' This rather improbable marriage of former adversaries was the logical step toward combating the underworld threat of assassination and abduction. The KGB have been successful in compiling masses of data on Mafia members, including their origins, contacts, crimes and, more to the point, the role they play. So far this information has only been used in the protection of vulnerable representatives, including their own. One attempt by Chechen rebels to abduct a prominent Russian envoy in Rostov was foiled when KGB officials ordered his bodyguard protection to be upgraded. Frustrated by the tightened security, the rebels immediately turned their attention to a civilian hospital, which they held until poorly trained security forces intervened, killing many of the hostages in the ensuing gun battle. It was one of the few occasions when bodyguards, deployed to save life, unknowingly caused a much greater loss.

The diplomatic card of immunity is a highly prized asset for any country with warlike tendencies, especially as the passage and safe conduct of the person holding such a card is enshrined in ancient rituals originating from the battlefields of the past. These rituals ensure that governments grant immunity to representatives of other countries and suffer the consequent inconvenience, but their own diplomats receive the same treatment and freedom in return.

Nowadays it is not unusual for some countries to use diplomats as part of their espionage machine, or even as initiators of war. History shows that some diplomats have made the latter option the only one left open to their governments, often in the belief that 'war is the continuation of diplomacy by other means'. However, it remains that the declaration of war terminates diplomacy until a victor emerges from the smouldering ashes of the battlefield.

Diplomatic discussions prior to hostilities are often a dangerous period for opposing mediators. The power of life and death that these diplomats possess can be far out of proportion to their own mediocre existence. No one would dispute that the assassination of diplomats involved in such negotiations would end the peace talks and hasten the advent of war, even if the deed was not committed by the opposing side but by a third party with a lot to gain from a conflict. It is dur-

Above: President Bill Clinton shakes hands with supporters while surrounded by Secret Service bodyguards. (Press Association)

Below: Personal Protection Officers from the former KGB Department 'A' stand within arm's reach of Lady Thatcher as she waves to a crowd in October Revolution Square in Kiev. (Press Association)

Above: When the US President meets the people his Secret Service protection team take no chances. Sunglasses are often worn to hide twitching eyes as they scan the crowd looking for danger. Bodyguards know only too well that what appears to be a camera-lens can so easily become a gun-barrel.

Below: A Royal Marine Close Protection Officer forms part of an outer security screen within yards of many heads of state. The use of military personnel to act as bodyguards is not unusual in Britain.

Above: One of the Queen's Personal Protection Team keeps in constant contact with the security advance party at the next location. Up-to-the-minute information is vital if the VIP is to be kept away from danger.

Below: The US Secret Service is not restricted to the United States. Here a bodyguard checks the area around St Paul's Cathedral in London before the arrival of the American Ambassador.

Above: The Israeli Police Minister Moshe Shahal tours Jerusalem's green line closely flanked by his *Shin Bet* bodyguard. Openly carrying weapons is now common-place for bodyguards in the Middle East, especially since the assassination of Yitzhak Rabin.

Left: Attorney Johnnie Cochran accompanied by his Muslim bodyguard arrives at the studios of CNN to appear on the Larry King show. Note the bulge under the body-guards coat, a sure and deliberate sign that a weapon is being carried. (Associated Press)

Above: An undercover Close Protection Officer sits watching the crowd outside Buckingham Palace. He hardly receives a second glance from passers by, despite the fact that concealed beneath his shirt is a communications receiver so that he can listen in to the 'security net', and a deadly SIG P226 9mm semi-automatic pistol. Also note the long hair which conveniently conceals his otherwise obvious ear-piece and tubing.

Below: Apart from the undercover officers watching the crowd from within, these Scotland Yard officers also watch, and photograph, the crowd from their high vantage point.

Above: A sniper from the Metropolitan Police's D11 firearms team occupies a counter-sniper position high above the 1995 VE Day celebrations in London. One of the lessons learnt from President Kennedy's assassination was that security agencies must command every high point.

Below: The first picture ever published of a Counter Assault Team vehicle. Hidden away from the public's view, these darkened windows conceal eight black-clad and heavily armed soldiers from the Special Air Service Regiment, ready to move into action and 'take out' would-be assassins. In the foreground is the Prime Minister's bodyguard and motorcade; and note the communications vehicle – complete with mast – parked rear left.

Right: Two motorcycle outriders from the British Prime Minister's Special Escort Group take a break during their very busy schedule.

Right: The world of private protection as many of us see it. Here bodyguards from Global Perspectives await the return of their military VIP.

Right: A female bodyguard is put through her paces during realistic firearms training. But very few will make it through to the world of close protection.

Above: Rajiv Gandhi had one of the tightest security screens of any of the world's VIPs. Despite this, he and his entourage of bodyguards were assassinated by a suicide bomber. (*Calcutta Times*)

Below: Lady Thatcher, one of the highest security risks, receives twenty-four hour protection from Scotland Yard. Her personal protection is provided by Special Branch (SO12). On the left is Detective Constable Chris Strickland; on the right, Detective Chief Inspector Barry Strevens.

ing this period, known as the transition to war, that bodyguards play a significant, vital and influential role. Here government bodyguards are at their most powerful. As outsiders they, and they alone, can wield the external influence that can halt the peace talks indefinitely. To do so would be hazardous, and might be misinterpreted by the other side. Because there is no room for error, those chosen to accompany peace mediators are not picked at random. They have proved to be the very best and are totally unflappable. Their vast experience and wide range of contacts within worldwide intelligence agencies open channels that provide the latest data, especially on the opposing side's military activity. This includes satellite reconnaissance photographs and ground-deployed 'human intelligence' sources. This may appear excessive and beyond the scope of ordinary bodyguards, but these are no ordinary bodyguards. It is imperative for them to know what the opposition is doing militarily, so as to gauge the danger their client is in at all times.

During the Gulf War, peace negotiators working behind the scenes in Baghdad were chaperoned by an entourage of personal protection officers, many of whom were better briefed on Iraqi troop deployment in Kuwait than the negotiators themselves. At no time, however, did the bodyguards volunteer this information, even in private, as it would have been considered 'unprofessional'.

The recent crisis in the former Yugoslavia created more diplomatic activity than was seen in any other area for decades. The daily scurry of United Nations peace negotiators from one warring faction to another, with bodyguards in tow, left most observers bewildered and beleaguered, for the mediators faced not two bitter sides but several. However, United Nations bodyguards faced the greatest task of all; protecting the envoys everyone wanted dead, when all sides had the military power to do the deed. In Bosnia there were no set rules to ensure adequate protection. Each day brought its own diplomatic timetable that changed by the hour. Attempting to conduct advance reconnaissance of motorcade routes and buildings was almost impossible. So, too, was the vetting of those with whom the mediators were compelled to negotiate, as they too changed hourly.

During the hostage crisis, when the Bosnian Serbs took United Nations troops hostage in late 1995, shuttle diplomacy by the Russians played a critical part in gaining the release of the soldiers. Yet they chose to take no bodyguard protection. Whether this was a deliberate show of trust or because they were assured no harm would come to their mediators can only be surmised. The fact that no Russian soldiers were taken prisoner, and the subsequent release of those held captive, were certainly indications to Western security agencies of the influence that Moscow had over the warring group. But other peace envoys, including religious and political mediators visiting Palé, have not been without their heavy blanket of personal protection, many of the negotiations being conducted amid tight security.

Diplomatic talks have always been private matters, held away from the glare of the world's mass media. This is a vital necessity if both sides are to generate and propose controversial ideas that would, if watched by the media, not normally be promoted for fear they could not be withdrawn. One of the roles of close-protection teams is to ensure that these meetings remain private, by debugging the rooms in advance and removing all communication facilities, including telephones and radios, except personal radios used by the bodyguards.

During negotiations there is normally a third party acting as an intermediary, generally from a neutral country with wide-ranging influential power. Recently the USA has been actively involved in successful intermediary work, especially in the Middle East, Africa, Korea and Northern Ireland, albeit in a limited way. Depending on the threat assessment, intermediaries will rarely accept bodyguard protection, the exception being the Archbishop of Canterbury's special envoy, Terry Waite, who was given a six-man, British-trained Druze bodyguard during his negotiations in Beirut. Yet in the end he too, like other intermediaries, had no protection at the vital moment. This is often because neutral mediators wish to appear impartial in the hope of gaining the trust of both sides. Sometimes this works, and sometimes it does not.

Abuse of diplomatic status has become a regular occurrence, particularly by those states determined to destabilise other governments.

Iran, Iraq and Libya have all been offenders in helping terrorist groups to commit crimes, and much of this support has come via diplomatic channels. Some diplomats have even gone to the extreme of committing terrorist acts of violence while shielded by diplomatic immunity. In April 1984 the staff of the Libyan People's Bureau in London opened fire on a peaceful demonstration, killing Yvonne Fletcher, a female police officer in the Metropolitan Police. The perpetrators were later allowed to leave the country unhindered, no doubt with the weapon hidden inside the official 'diplomatic bag', which cannot be opened or searched. For law-abiding countries this is a critical necessity for confidential communication between government and embassies, but for those prepared to flout immunity agreements it is just another way of abusing their privileges.

Some countries are not as blatant when it comes to terrorist crime, but their involvement is strong all the same. In late 1986 the staff of the Syrian embassy in London was caught red-handed and implicated by a British court as accessories to an attempt to blow up an Israeli El Al Boeing 747. No charges were brought owing to their diplomatic immunity, but the British government had no hesitation in expelling the ambassador and his entire staff, and severing all relations with Damascus.

Such actions have caused diplomats in general to lose the respect they once had. Mistrust and suspicion may be the reason why bodyguard protection is now required, and only recently have these feelings started to fade. Only time will tell whether the world of diplomacy will ever regain its credibility. The fact that diplomats, rather than politicians, are now the most likeliest of the world's VIPs to be assassinated has not gone unnoticed, particularly by those who wait patiently in the darkened wings. For it is the bodyguards who will bear the responsibility for the protection of diplomacy and, ultimately, future world peace.

6

For Queen and Country

While politicians insist on maintaining the tightest of security screens available for the world's VIPs, members of the Royal Family are not prepared to be shackled by security or bound by their bodyguards, even if they are the world's prime targets for assassination and abduction. In recent years a number of sporadic security scares have occurred during official visits abroad, but, while some have attracted massive media interest, like the attempted shooting of Prince Charles in 1994, others have hardly raised an eyebrow. Ever since the Provisional IRA killed Lord Mountbatten in 1979 (the only member of royalty to die at the hands of modern terrorism), security has been carefully stage-managed to conform to the Queen's insistence on an unobtrusive protection screen. Yet things are not always as they seem.

David Kang, a 23-year-old student, sat quietly in the front row of a jubilant crowd in Sydney's Tumbalong Park, Australia, awaiting the arrival of that ever-popular member of the Royal Family, Prince Charles. Kang was hardly noticed by the scores of uniformed and plain-clothed police officers, including a handful of Australian SAS covert protection officers drafted in to mingle with the crowd owing to the fear that anti-monarchy demonstrators might attempt to disrupt the visit. But as the Prince's motorcade arrived and the crowd stood cheering his arrival, one covert bodyguard noticed that Kang 'made no movement' and appeared 'transfixed to the stage'. The bodyguards considered this to be 'unusual at such an idyllic time'. The bodyguard from the New South Wales police added later: 'Alarm bells began to ring inside my head as I noted his lack of interest ... I moved to a position about two seats to his left and noticed his right hand move inside his trouser pocket ... I tried to get closer but was prevented from doing so by two bystanders ... I tried to push between them, but before I could do so he was on the stage.' This sudden movement took the security teams by surprise, leaving them in shock for a split second.

Jamine Cook, who was seated next to Kang, said: 'It happened very quickly, he was at the stage before I noticed.' Simultaneously, as the Prince stepped forward to give an Australia Day address, Kang rushed forward and fired two shots toward the Prince from no more than five feet. The Prince looked stunned but remained calm in the face of such impending danger, characteristically fiddling with his cufflinks throughout, a nervous habit he has had since adolescence. Within a split second of the second shot being fired Kang was floored by a scrum of covert protection officers and dignitaries while the Prince's personal protection officer, Superintendent Colin Trimmings, took up a protective stance between the Prince and Kang and inquired if he was all right. 'I am fine,' came the cool reply.

As the world's press tried frantically to catch up with events, David Kang was handcuffed and spirited away by plain-clothed police officers. Meanwhile, Trimmings removed the Prince to a discreet distance and suggested that perhaps he should leave. The Prince refused, and to the world's surprise and apparently unruffled by the incident, continued his address and was back shaking hands with the waiting public within half an hour, albeit with a much more visible and tighter security screen.

Only later did it emerge that the weapon had been a starting pistol loaded with blanks. Kang's motive for the attack was to highlight the treatment the Cambodian boat people were receiving from the Australian authorities (Kang was half Cambodian). He was charged with 'attacking an internationally protected person', which carried a maximum 20-year sentence, but in a surprise move he was released on condition he admitted himself to a psychiatric hospital for the treatment of severe depression.

The following day, commander Richard Aylard, the Prince's private secretary, stated: 'The Prince was disappointed that "one silly incident" could have damaged an otherwise good visit.' This apparent dismissal of the incident by Buckingham Palace failed to suppress the outcry and public bickering between the British and Australian security forces. Senior Australian officials, supported by New South Wales Police Minister Terry Griffiths, rejected the Palace's statement that 'the responsibility for security remains with the host government', complaining that the Palace had placed too many restrictions on their protective arrangements. In their defence they produced a Palace directive stating: 'There are to be no security forces between the Prince and the public.' At the time it was not known that the statement had been drafted at the Prince's personal request, after he had rejected Trimmings's recommendation that extra security personnel be used. This recommendation, made in light of British intelligence reports provided early that year, stated that demonstrators supporting the Australian Prime Minister's stance for a republic by the year 2000 could instigate disturbances, or even an assassination attempt, although the latter possibility was never really taken seriously by members of the Royalty Protection Squad.

As the public squabbling continued, New South Wales Premier John Fahey stated: 'It is important we re-evaluate what has occurred. We will have a debriefing to establish exactly what the person's movements were.' Yet for the rest of the visit security commanders drafted in an extra 50 close-protection officers, including more soldiers from their élite SAS regiment, much to the annoyance of the Prince.

One of the first security questions to be raised in the subsequent inquiry was why Kang had been allowed to get so close without being searched, and why no security barrier was erected in front of the stage. Australian close-protection teams argued that it would be impossible to implement a mechanism to search the public, especially given the potentially vast area the Prince could cover during one of his impromptu walkabouts or an unscheduled public address, and added that trying to vet every person who entered or left such an area would require far greater manpower than was currently available.

American bodyguards were unmoved by the smokescreen generated by their Australian counterparts, asserting that they had been far too relaxed towards the golden rules of personal protection, indicating as an example the close-protection officer who noticed Kang's strange behaviour before the attack. They pointed out that he had made no attempt to communicate a warning to other members of the security team, deciding instead to go it alone, contrary to all known standard operating procedures.

One British security source told the author: 'Luckily this time the shots were blanks fired as a desperate cry for help from a depressed young man, but if a determined terrorist decided on the same method the outcome would undoubtedly be fatal.'

Bodyguard protection for the Royal Family has always been a low-key affair, even dating back to the troubled times of Queen Victoria, who herself was the target of at least seven assassination attempts. The monarchy has only ever believed in one protector – God.

The monarchy's immense prestige and exposure to the world's media has made them prime targets for publicity-seeking loners and terrorists alike, though the latter have rarely chosen royalty as one of its main targets since the IRA killing of Lord Mountbatten in 1979. Though this did create media interest, it only served to turn the people against the IRA, which received massive condemnation, not only from Britain but also from their own following in the Province. The monarchy can no longer be considered a 'legitimate target' by the IRA, despite it being the figurehead of British rule.

The main threat still continues to present itself in the form of the mentally ill or depressed assailant hell-bent on attracting attention. Such persons still exist, as the attack on Prince Charles illustrates all too clearly, and many bodyguards believe that the British government's decision to cut down on the number of psychiatric hospitals, releasing sick patients into the community, can only lead to an increase in the risk to VIPs from assassination. Since this policy was implemented, in 1991, Buckingham Palace has reported 30 breaches of security, from the common one of climbing the perimeter fence to the more serious ramming of the two-ton wrought-iron gates with vehicles. Despite the fact that these breaches have been successfully intercepted before the 'inner sanctum' of the Palace was entered, many protection officers have recently expressed concern for the increasing problem. They admit, however, that royal protection is as tight as the Palace will allow it to get.

The security that protects members of the Royal Family has improved greatly over the last two decades, but such improvements only came about after serious threats. One such threat occurred when

Princess Anne was confronted by an assailant determined to kidnap her for a ransom of £3 million in 1974. He failed, but the incident could not be swept under the carpet. It was the most serious attack ever undertaken against the Royal Family and prompted a reassessment of British security.

On 20 March 1974, as Princess Anne and her husband Captain Mark Phillips neared Buckingham Palace, their armoured limousine was shunted by a car and forced to stop. Inside the vehicle was 26-year-old Ian Ball. The Princess's bodyguard, Inspector Jim Beaton, and her Palace chauffeur, Alexander Callender, stepped from the vehicle to check the damage, not realising Ball's true intentions. In the mêlée that followed Ball opened fire with a 0.22-calibre pistol, hitting both Beaton and Callender in the chest at point-blank range. Beaton retreated to the rear of the limousine, pulled his Walther self-loading pistol and attempted to chamber a round, but due to extreme fatigue caused by shock and loss of blood he discharged the weapon accidentally, hitting and shattering the limousine's rear windscreen and spraying glass over Anne and Mark Phillips as they desperately fought with Ball to prevent him taking the Princess. Beaton struggled to the side door, where Ball was standing, raised his weapon and fired, but heard the fatal 'dead man's click' as the weapon jammed. Ball turned and ordered the bodyguard to drop his weapon, and Beaton, knowing it was all but useless, did so. Then in an act of sheer bravery he jumped between Ball and the Princess. Ball fired, hitting the detective again. Unperturbed, Beaton scrambled into the vehicle as Ball noticed a passing policemen, Michael Hills, and a journalist, John McConnell, running to help. The young constable radioed the incident to Scotland Yard; the first time it was officially recorded. Ball raised his weapon, shot them both, and returned his attention to the Princess. Her bodyguard, by now succumbing to his near-fatal wounds, made one last grab for the kidnapper's weapon and was shot a third time, falling to the floor unconscious.

Ronald Russell, a passing taxicab driver, now entered the fracas and punched Ball in the head. Ball turned and fired, hitting the taxi's side window. From all around came the wail of sirens as police cars converged on the spot from all directions, bringing a mass of rein-forcements. Ball, seeing that the odds were now stacked against him, made a run for it toward St James's Palace, where he was floored by Detective Constable Peter Edwards, who disarmed and handcuffed the screaming assailant.

Ball was no amateur, and had made serious plans and prepara-tions to kidnap the Princess. He had rented a house in Fleet, Hamp-shire, under an alias and stocked it with enough food for several weeks' isolation. One room had been modified to include the attach-ment of chains to a wall, and the windows were sealed from the inside. Ball made one damaging admission during police questioning, stating that he had followed the Princess for some weeks before the attempt, and notes were found at the house containing times, dates and places to confirm this. Yet none of this surveillance was noticed by her rota-tion of bodyguards. Ball was later detained indefinitely under the Mental Health Act of 1959.

In recognition of his courage, Inspector Beaton was awarded the George Cross and later became the Queen's personal bodyguard. Ronald Russell and PC Michael Hills were both awarded George Medals, while Alexander Callender and John McConnell were each awarded the Queen's Gallantry Medal.

The Queen and Prince Philip were on an official visit to Indone-sia when the Duke of Edinburgh was woken in the early hours of the morning to be told the news. He elected to wait until morning to relay the news to his wife, so as not to alarm her. Yet the incident was bound to come as a shock, and officials admitted some days later that the Queen was 'shaken' by the news. Steps were immediately taken and a noticeable escalation of royal protection was soon visible to the trained eye.

The changes were not limited to royal protection. Scotland Yard's protective resources would never be the same again. Body-guards detailed with royal protection duties and under the adminis-trative control of the Yard's 'A' Squad were regrouped into the Royalty Protection Branch and given the additional cover of a mobile protec-tion screen provided by a fleet of motorcycle escorts manned by the

Special Escort Group. In response to the failure of the pistol, protection officers were issued with the Smith & Wesson 0.38 Special short-barrelled revolver. The government, known for their determination not to waste money, passed the consignment of Walthers to the prison service in Northern Ireland, who received them with as much enthusiasm as those who had given them up. Branch bodyguards also received the first formal training in how to handle firearms by a newly formed unit of firearms specialists known as D11.

One advantage the revolver had over its predecessor was the ability to clear a stoppage quickly, just by squeezing the trigger, whereas if the pistol misfired it was necessary to pull back the slide to eject the round before another could enter the chamber. If a bodyguard was suffering from fatigue brought about by gunshot wounds or serious injuries, it made clearing the stoppage all the more difficult, and, taking into account the time confrontations lasted, bodyguards had precious little time to spare.

However, a revolver was not the ideal solution to the problem. For a start it was much bulkier than a pistol to carry, making it more difficult to conceal from a public wholly against its police carrying firearms. The pistol could also be easily slipped into a shoulder holster which allowed the bodyguard easy access when needed, whereas the revolver's size ruled this out (although some officers tried), forcing it to be worn at the rear of the hip-belt, which made its withdrawal in a confrontation while seated in a car all but impossible. However, the development of 'mini' revolvers which still have the velocity to stop a man with the first two shots has largely eradicated these problems, even if the British police refuse to use them.

On the other hand, worldwide military special forces detailed with personal protection have continuously used self-loading pistols such as the 9mm Browning high-powered semi-automatic handgun and its replacement, the Glock 18, a lightweight weapon with a magazine capacity of 17, 19 or 33 rounds. Both provide soldiers with maximum firepower and devastating accuracy within the shortest time-frame, three essential requirements needed to keep themselves and their clients alive.

106

So why did police bodyguards not just swap the pistols for these more powerful and reliable weapons? Simply because they were not allowed to, mainly because the law of minimum force determined the weapons they could or could not use. As we have seen elsewhere, commanders who requested the use of military bodyguards first had to justify the high loss of life that might result if the soldiers were called upon to open fire. The question was: 'Is he at sufficient risk to warrant such a loss?' The answer then, and now, is often no. Commanders naturally turned to the easier solution of issuing police bodyguards with single-shot weapons, and reinforced their operational procedures by adopting a clause that ran something like this: 'Officers are permitted to return fire only if they believe their, or their charge's life is in immediate danger and shots have been fired.'

Training police bodyguards to hold their fire was, and still is, no easy task, especially in some Middle Eastern countries where the emphasis has always swayed towards shoot first, ask questions and apologise later. In time, however, British and Australian police bodyguards saw their weapons only as 'a last resort', which was exactly what the instructors had hoped for.

The main improvement in royalty protection came not from within the police force, but from the use of an outside agency. During the following year secret plans were prepared and instigated for the SAS to provide training 'demonstrations' for members of the Royal Family and their bodyguards. Admittedly this was not a new idea; the Queen and Prince Philip had both watched such exhibitions before. The difference now was that the Royal Family were expected to take part in this realistic training, in the hope that it would prepare them for the reality of an attack. The idea, thought up by an enterprising young major who would eventually aspire to command the regiment, was endorsed by Princess Anne, who became its first guinea-pig.

On a wet Sunday afternoon in a deserted 'Fighting in a Built-up Area' training complex on the regiment's exercise area near Hereford, the Princess's armoured limousine slowed to a stop for a mock royal visit. In attendance were her personal protection officers, a mobile escort and royal aides. The mock crowd was made up of cardboard cut-outs of other members of the Royal Family, which raised a smile from the Princess as she stepped from the vehicle and walked towards the glassless building. As she did so, the silence was shattered by an explosion to her right, followed by a short burst of automatic gunfire. Her personal bodyguard unceremoniously pushed the Princess's head down and turned her back towards the car in one flowing movement. Simultaneously, other bodyguards returned fire (with blanks) at the two black-clad figures who would become world famous after the Iranian Embassy siege rescue. A second burst of automatic gunfire followed, and the Princess was pushed into the vehicle and immediately joined by an aide and her bodyguard, who continued to resist the Princess's insistence to look up at the chaos raging in the street. Another explosion and more gunfire was the driver's unrehearsed cue to engage gear and withdraw. As the limousine screeched away, the Princess's guardian inquired if she was hurt and received the fiery reply: 'No, but the person who pinched my bottom has a lot to answer for.' Such realistic exercises are great preparatory training for both the royal VIPs and their bodyguards, and every member of the Royal Family except the Queen and the Duke of Edinburgh have taken part in one or several exercises since their creation.

The Queen has always insisted on low-key unobtrusive protection, preferring bodyguards to stay in the background and out of sight so that she is not hindered by security protocol when meeting the people, unlike the President of the USA, who is begrudgingly forced to accept his imposed posse of guardians. Royal security is unique insofar as it is designed with the Queen's personal wishes in mind. Her reaction to the improvements during 1974-5 are not recorded, but security advisers claimed at the time that 'the new implementations have Her Majesty's full support'.

Another problem facing security chiefs, now that personal protection was the best it was going to be for some time at least, was how to ensure the Queen's safety at her private residence of Buckingham Palace, undoubtedly the most famous building in the world. All the normal security arrangements were in place: high fences, television cameras and guards, including ceremonial troops from the Foot Guards and Household Cavalry. But minor breaches of security still caused commanders at Scotland Yard much concern, mainly by over-eager tourists determined to climb the outer perimeter fence, or the occasional demonstrator keen to undermine police authority. One police chief, commenting in 1979, said: 'It is only a matter of time before someone gains access to the Palace itself.' His concerns were brushed aside by fellow colleagues as paranoia verging on the ridiculous.

They had a point. The Palace already had the most advanced security system of any of the country's state buildings. Not only was the outer fence covered by cameras, there was also a series of microwave-beam (later replaced by laser-beam) detectors placed strategically all the way back to the walls of the main building. All windows and doors were fitted with security locks only accessible from the inside, and were covered by movement sensors linked to audible alarms in the control centre. Key areas throughout the Palace, such as corridor junctions and stairways forming the arteries of the building, were fitted with pressure pads concealed beneath carpets, and each of the private rooms was furnished with panic buttons connected to the control centre.

But such security devices are only as good as the men in the nerve centre, detailed to respond if the alarms are activated. Police officers detailed to man the control centre would often switch off, reset, or at worse totally ignore the visual and audio warnings. This attitude derived from the countless false alarms, most notably from the microwave detectors, which were positioned so low that any roaming animals could easily set them off.

These faults and the police commander's prediction made front-page news with the banner headline 'Intruder at the Queen's Bedside' in July 1982. The story was only reported because an eagle-eyed court journalist had heard the charges brought against the intruder, Michael Fagan. The government, still with its mind on the Falklands Conflict, had made no comment in a deliberate attempt to stop the story from leaking and, ultimately, to lessen their embarrassment. Some hours later, however, William Whitelaw, the then Home Secretary, admitted in a statement that Buckingham Palace's security was still 'not satisfactory'.

Michael Fagan's intrusion at the Palace was not his first. Some hours before he entered the Queen's bedroom he had climbed up a drainpipe to a first-floor window and slid it open, setting off the light detector in the control centre in the process. A security officer patrolling nearby rooms was ordered to check the area but Fagan, hearing the guard approaching, closed the window and retreated down to a nearby wall. The guard reported 'nothing unusual ... just another false alarm', which was noted in the 'action taken' column of the night log book, and continued his rounds.

Fagan returned at 6.40 a.m. and again entered through the same window. Whether the alarm was activated is not recorded in the log book; one can surmise that it was, but was assumed to be another false alarm and ignored. Fagan was now standing within the office of the Master of the Queen's Household, where he took off his sandals and socks. After rummaging through drawers he explored the adjoining rooms unchallenged, cutting his thumb on a broken ashtray in the process, before tiptoeing upstairs to the Queen's private quarters, walking across two pressure pads as he did so, both of which had been switched off by the duty controller soon after the Palace cleaners had arrived. Fagan then walked past both cleaners, who mistook him for a builder working in another area of the Palace. How he came to choose the Queen's bedroom door out of all the other alarmed doors leading from the corridor, including Prince Philip's bedroom, which he had to pass, has never been answered. What is known is that at 7.16 a.m. the Queen realised a stranger was in her chambers, and in fear pressed the panic button to the control centre. There was no response; the Queen should have heard a reply ring informing her that officers were on the way.

It emerged later that the police in the control centre were preparing to come off shift, and were not immediately available in the alarm room. Receiving no reply, and with Fagan approaching her bedside, she immediately pressed the bedside bell, which rang in the corridor. However, her Special Branch bodyguard had gone off duty some time earlier and had been replaced by a Palace footman, who incidentally had not yet returned from walking the corgis. The Queen realised she was alone and with no immediate help, and as Fagan made small talk she lifted the telephone receiver, dialled 222 for the Palace operator and said calmly: 'Send a police officer.' The operator in turn relayed this message to the control centre (it was timed at 7.18 a.m.), but again the police failed to react. Six minutes elapsed as the Queen and Fagan spoke about Prince Charles and her earlier brush with death during the Trooping of the Colour, when a 17-year-old named Marcus Sergeant shot six blank cartridges from a starting pistol. He was brought down by covert bodyguards and ceremonial soldiers.

The Queen, by now disturbed at the lack of response, called for assistance after leading Fagan into the corridor on the promise of cigarettes from the pantry, and instructed a chambermaid, Elizabeth Andrew, who was arriving to wake her, to take him there. Seconds later her footman returned, turned into the corridor, and in dazed bewilderment saw Fagan and made a grab at him, helped by the feisty corgis, who had decided to join the affray. Moments later police officers arrived on the stairs. Seeing the Queen they began to tidy themselves, much to her irritation, and she shouted: 'Come on, get a bloody move on.' Seconds later Fagan was manhandled away and arrested.

It was not long before questions were raised in Parliament and the tabloid press regarding the apparently lax security. Within weeks a commission of inquiry was set up by commanders of the Royal Protection Squad to find the security flaws. They did not have to look hard, and within a matter of days Palace police officers were either 'transferred' or 'retired'. Fagan's means of entry into the Palace was quickly identified and a number of improvements were made, including the use of a new slippery paint on all drainpipes, an idea previously vetoed by bureaucrats in the Environment Department as too costly. Police officers on duty in the control centre admitted that they did not rush to the Queen's aid after she had telephoned the operator because 'the operator reported the Queen sounded calm'. But the real reason for the delay was revealed to the author by a police source some years later: 'Given the time of day and past experience, they feared they would have to take the corgis for a walk ... a task that was often requested of them.'

One major improvement that was not fully exploited by security patrols had actually been enforced six months before the Fagan intrusion, and in direct response to the Iran Embassy siege. Soon after black-clad figures had abseiled from the embassy roof to rescue hostages from the hands of Iranian terrorists, SAS security advisers visited the Palace and other notable buildings to make detailed plans of the internal arrangements of each room, including measurements of the exact position, to the nearest inch, of all furniture, doors, windows and staircases. Knowledge of the exact layout of a building is imperative to hostage rescue teams, but it can also be of immense value to bodyguards and security personnel the world over if used correctly. The SAS requested that strict guidelines be implemented, forbidding staff to rearrange the furniture without prior notice to the regiment, no matter how small the object.

Top-level bodyguards working in such buildings now use these plans to become familiar with the building, and after an initial familiarisation period a bodyguard is able to enter a room and quickly identify changes. This can be of particular value at night, when most intrusions occur and when few members of the household are awake. However, police officers on duty that night failed to use this to their advantage. Had they done so, they would have realised that someone had entered the building. During the inquiry it emerged that on Fagan's first visit he had pushed to a nearby wall a large leather chair that blocked his entrance through the window; the police had failed to notice this.

The year 1982 proved to be an exhausting one for the Queen and her security team, as scare after scare presented itself both at home, with the Trooping of the Colour shooting and Fagan's intrusions, and abroad, where another attempted shooting captured the headlines.

The incident occurred when the Queen made an official visit to Dunedin, on New Zealand's South Island. An inventive if immature 17-year-old, Christopher Lewis, and two other boys stole an 0.22-calibre rifle and took up what happened to be a good firing position within an office rented by a friend's father. Lewis, determined to form his own terrorist group and with the Queen as the first target, chose a downward trajectory toward the local university, where the Queen was due to go on a public walkabout. As Her Majesty entered the rifle's sights, he fired. Bodyguards and personal aides close to her heard the shot, but made no effort to shield her. Only her personal protection officer, Michael Trestrail, made any noticeable movement toward her. But when a second shot failed to follow, Trestrail backed off and the walkabout continued without further incident.

Lewis, annoyed that the round had fallen short owing to the low calibre of the rifle, stormed out of the building in a rage. Police officers, totally unaware of the incident, later arrested Lewis and his two accomplices during an armed robbery. In custody Lewis blurted out, 'I nearly got her', and the full story emerged. Australian security personnel present at the walkabout confirmed the story, but did not immediately inform Trestrail at Buckingham Palace. He was told later by a third party in passing, much to his annoyance. Not surprisingly, relations between the Palace's security team and its Australian counterparts became strained for some time, and things were not helped when it was admitted that Lewis had escaped from a secure psychiatric hospital shortly before a visit by Prince Charles. Security advisers to the Palace recommended that the Prince of Wales's tour of the country should be cancelled, but the Prince refused. A compromise was reached when it was agreed that the Palace would inform the Australian authorities that the visit would not proceed unless Lewis was behind bars. The threat was taken seriously, and within 48 hours Lewis was back in custody and remained in a maximum security prison for the duration of the Prince's tour. Needless to say, relations between the two protection agencies improved somewhat after the visit. However, the strain of such a turbulent period proved too much for the Queen, and at the end of the year she took an unusual seven-week vacation, the longest in her reign to date.

Persuading a VIP of the importance of bodyguards can sometimes be a futile task, especially when that individual happens to be the British Sovereign, who detests undue fuss and responds to her protection officers' frequent speeches about the threat of death with the mortal and frustrating words 'so be it'. This attitude has been typical of monarchies through the ages. Their belief that the Almighty is the sole controller of their fate leaves many of their bodyguards speechless, but will never change despite historical proof to support the bodyguard's argument. This proof includes the turmoil during the executions of Tsar Nicholas II in 1917, and the death of Lord Mountbatten over six decades later. They have ordered better protection for their offspring, even if it has been rejected, but the trend of going it alone and relying on God's hand to guide will continue for many years.

Nevertheless, those responsible for royal protection are not allowed such faith to indulge in the royal optimism that the people will do them no harm. The one man with the burden of the Queen's security on his shoulders is Inspector Penrice, an elegant and sage bodyguard with the demeanour of a member of the Bar but the watchfulness of a lion stalking its prey. His vast experience of personal protection spans nearly two decades, working under such notable figures as Inspector Michael Trestrail (Queen's personal bodyguard, 1973–82), and his replacement Jim Beaton, GC (1982–9). Penrice became a favourite with the Queen because of his courteous and tactful approach to her protection, showing a deep understanding of her feelings about security. He changed the emphasis from a highly visible presence to an invisible protection screen, using covert bodyguards placed strategically at key points within the crowd or acting as photo journalists to snap the crowd for later analysis by intelligence experts to identify the recurring face. Such decoys conduct their intelligence gathering with hardly a second glance from the oblivious media or public surrounding them.

Being the Queen's personal bodyguard brings with it a great deal of notoriety, fame that can work for or against the bodyguard depending on his personality and attitude toward the media. The fact that the tabloid press are prepared to pay heavily for a 'royal scoop' makes the bodyguard's personal life all the more dangerous. From the moment he is ordained into the protection of royalty, his life will be scrutinised by eager researchers conducting an endless search for ammunition for their newspaper's guns.

Michael Trestrail is such a case, and the highest ranking body-guard to succumb to Fleet Street. As the Queen's personal bodyguard, well respected by both Her Majesty and the Duke of Edinburgh, he resigned soon after allegations began to spread that he was involved in a homosexual love affair. His lover, 36-year-old male prostitute Michael Rauch, had offered to sell his story to a Fleet Street newspaper, but was arrested by Scotland Yard before the story was published. Trestrail confessed to the affair and, although the Queen was happy for him to stay, his removal was inevitable. It was a sad end to the career of a bodyguard who had done much to improve royal security throughout the 1970s.

The press has unlimited power, and can damage promising careers purely out of envy or dislike. As a veteran of royal protection explains: 'In recent years the press has become more determined to seek out a story, no matter how small or insignificant it may be, and some will go to any lengths to obtain a story or take compromising photographs.' He continues: 'Due to the closeness and knowledge bodyguards have of their clients' movements and unofficial visits, detectives assigned to protective duties around the Royal Family have become the target of the eager journalist, hell-bent on obtaining the inside story that could lead to the next front page exclusive.'

For this reason royal bodyguards have learned to remain tight-lipped while at the same time not appearing to brush off or ignore the constant barrage of questions, as this could prove counterproductive. Such actions could cause a great deal of undue attention from a spurned journalist with the power to produce front-page news, whether it is true or not.

Unscrupulous journalists are fully aware that close-protection officers detailed to royalty protection are bound by their oath of silence and are unable to speak out publicly over any allegations that may appear in print. This gives the tabloids the freedom to publish any story they like about bodyguards' 'closeness' to their royal VIPs, as they know that the bodyguard is unlikely to deny or admit the report. Bodyguards working for high-profile figures who are the subject of media attention, such as the Prince and Princess of Wales during their amicable separation, find themselves constantly in the public goldfish-bowl, where upsetting a journalist could cause a far greater embarrassment than if they were to lose their principals by assassination.

Overseas security, as already shown, can be a cumbersome and traumatic experience for both the guardian and guarded, regardless of meticulous advance planning by the Palace, especially as the Queen or Prince Charles can expect to be abroad for at least three months of the year on official visits to every corner of the globe. British bodyguards still cringe when they remember how the Queen was mobbed by a crowd of well-wishers when she visited a shanty town in South Africa. The host government's head of security had assured the Royalty Protection Branch some months before that there was no risk involved in a visit to such a volatile area. Reluctantly, Branch bodyguards agreed and authorised an official walkabout, a mistake that became apparent when close-protection officers were powerless to keep the enthusiastic crowds at bay. The Queen showed her concern when the path was blocked, and calmly turned to Penrice and enquired: 'Which way should we go?' His reply is not known, but the Queen was visibly reassured and a path was soon cleared to her waiting emergency back-up vehicle, a Range Rover, which moments earlier had contained her personal physician, nurse, and medical resuscitation equipment.

Official overseas visits by members of the Royal Family are organised months in advance and meticulously planned. A team consisting of the Assistant Secretary to the Queen, her Press Secretary and a senior member of the Royalty Protection Branch visit the country concerned to gather as much information as possible, including potential venues, motorcade routes, flight arrangements, dining facilities and whether Buckingham Palace cooks are required to attend. At this stage no firm arrangements will be made with the host government so far as a schedule for the visit is concerned, but they are consulted regarding the places they would like the Queen to visit. After the team's return to the UK, an informal meeting is held with the Queen and Prince Philip to decide on a final schedule. Not all of the team's suggested venues will be agreed by Her Majesty, and the security team may 'advise' that a particular locality is not a security-viable choice.

Bodyguards and security advisers at this level need to have the most exceptional skills of diplomacy and tact. A royal bodyguard told the author: 'The Queen does not take too kindly to being told what to do.' The majority of the chosen venues, whoever decides upon them, pose few real problems to a switched-on protection team, including the Royal Family's. With time and resources on their side they can negotiate with the host government and devise a contingency plan for any eventuality. The Queen is rarely aware of the security around her, or the procedures in place to keep her alive. This is not born of ignorance, but is due to the fact that she has lived inside the cocoon of protective security all her life, and will do so until she dies. Members of royalty know no other way of life, and bodyguards become all but a part of the wallpaper, just like the royal courtiers and equerries. This actually is of benefit to the personal protection officer, allowing him a great deal more flexibility in planning local or long-distance journeys.

Although the Queen is informed of her daily routine of events and given general timings, she has no knowledge of how, or by which route, she will travel. This allows her bodyguards to make even the most dangerous of trips complicated but secure. They will rarely choose the most obvious route, and never travel without the Special Escort Group consisting of three motorcycle outriders, but even they are not told of the route until minutes before departure. The problem is much more complicated when the Queen is abroad, and improvisation often plays an important part. Some countries, such as Australia, Canada and New Zealand, are frequently visited by the Royal Family and so have specialist police units able to provide similar facilities to those provided by the British police. But some tours are a security nightmare for bodyguards, and stretch the team's patience to the limit. Namibia in 1990 and Malta two years later are two recent examples where no police escort vehicles were available and no additional covert protection personnel were employed. Royal Marine Commandos had to be flown in from warships patrolling in the Mediterranean to fill the undercover gap.

Despite the contingency plans operated by the royal security team, things do go wrong. The official walkabout poses the greatest security risk, in particular the impromptu 'meeting of the people' for which the Queen is renowned. It is a habit she rarely indulges in now, much to the pleasure of her bodyguards, but one that her son Prince Charles seems to have adopted, especially in Australia.

Persuading royalty not to undertake walkabouts is a futile task for bodyguards, whereas Prime Ministers are all too willing to agree with their security advisers and are happiest conversing with the public through the medium of the television, particularly in today's climate of public hostility. The monarchy, on the other hand, is publicly financed rather than publicly elected, and naturally the British taxpayer expects the Royal Family to be accessible as far as is practical. The Queen and her family are fully aware of this, and do their best to accommodate the adoring royalists, but do so while remaining within the bounds of state security.

There are, of course, limitations to the Queen's powers regarding her own accessibility. She may wish to meet the people of the Commonwealth during overseas visits, but if her bodyguards have decided in advance that it would be unwise to expose her to undue risk, all temptations will be carefully removed. This will include positioning the crowds in such a way that it becomes all but impossible for the Queen to talk to them. Even though she is a head of state, she certainly has limited powers over the fine detail of public walkabouts and, although she may later complain to her personal protection officer or head of security, the threat has been averted and the Palace bodyguards are quite happy to apologise for any 'misunderstanding'. 'I would prefer to apologise to a living Queen than to a nation mourning an assassinated monarch', is how one bodyguard put it.

Public walkabouts are conducted in a joyous atmosphere of buoyant joviality. However, the more observant onlooker will see, lurking in the background and on the shoulder of the Queen, the dapper, suited figures of personal protection officers, who rarely smile or avert their eyes from the crowd as they scan robotically from left to right. Every sudden movement is spotted and assessed in a split second for its threat potential. Who is to know that the next raised hand will not contain a pistol, hand-grenade or knife, or that the supposedly harmless camera flash could be a fatal muzzle-spark from a pistol fired from the crowd?

The unpredictability of crowds during walkabouts poses the ultimate dilemma for bodyguards. None of the massed crowd can be scrutinised or purified by protection teams in advance to ensure maximum security, and they come from a variety of backgrounds not immediately apparent to the personal protection officer on the ground. Admittedly, the majority of the people are there in the hope that they might see, no matter how briefly, the Royal Family; a memory many will cherish for all time. However, bodyguards are looking for the minority that could cause a problem or, even worse, attempt assassination, something that has not been done since the killing of Lord Mountbatten by the IRA in 1979. Surprisingly, terrorism has been the least of the threats to the British Monarchy since the above-mentioned killing. The IRA had intended to strike at the heart of British rule to prove to the government that it was a force to be reckoned with, but by killing a national war hero who was a loved member of the Royal Family the IRA lost much support. Lord Mountbatten was an easy target by anyone's standards. He refused to heed his bodyguards' advice and eluded their protective cover by playing hide and seek in the Irish countryside he knew so well. He was a favourite uncle of Prince Charles, and they spent much time together while at Buckingham Palace. It has been reported that Charles was so deeply affected by his uncle's assassination that he has never really come to terms with the killing.

Today, terrorism would play no part in an attempt to assassinate members of the British Royal Family, though that is not to say that they are the only exclusive élite outside the scope of the sniper's rifle. Quite the contrary. For example, killing the Queen Mother could never be justified to a populace prepared to accept random violence as a daily norm. Nevertheless, other monarchs are susceptible to terrorist assassins, but only if the opportunity is provided.

During the summer of 1995 three alleged members of a Basque terrorist movement, Juan José Rego, his son Inake Rego and a close friend, Jorge Garcia Sertucha, were arrested by the Spanish counter-terrorist unit, the GEO, in an apartment near King Juan Carlos's Marivent Palace overlooking the royal motor yacht *Fortuna*. All three were suspected of planning the assassination of the king or members of the Jordanian and Greek royal families. To support their theory police found a highly sophisticated sniper's rifle, complete with telescopic sights and a silencer, in the apartment, and they later recovered a further three hand pistols, two sub-machine pistols and a large quantity of Semtex explosive from a second address. In the following days a further nine people were arrested in Spain and France in a joint operation with the French SDECE.

Documentation found on Sertucha at the time of his arrest indicated that the Royal Family, and Prince Talal of Jordan, who was visiting them at the time, had indeed been under covert surveillance for some months by the terrorist group. It was not revealed whether the king's personal protection team had noticed this surveillance, but the fact that security was tightened and a review was implemented immediately afterwards suggests they had not.

Incidents as serious as this against many members of royalty are rare. However, the event highlights the fact that the 'preventive' capability implemented in the 1970s is operating to a much higher standard, and co-operation between Europe's security forces and intelligence has improved dramatically. Yet no matter how good it gets, the lone crank is still out there, and provides the greatest threat. As seen earlier, security improvements can only go so far in preventing an attack, and although there are fewer would-be lone assassins lurking in the shadows, they have not totally disappeared.

Media hype surrounding an incident when a cyclist rode through a security cordon and asked Princess Diana for a kiss was somewhat exaggerated. One royal bodyguard present at the time later said: 'It's stupid, at no time was the Princess in any danger. The man was watched intently by us as he approached her, and if he had made any attempt to reach for a weapon he would have been stopped immediately.' 'What many journalists don't realise,' he added, 'is that the Princess insists on being "a free spirit"; they're her words not ours, and she has always insisted on minimal protection because she enjoys meeting the public. Further to that I would add, that as bodyguards we cannot brandish weapons every time someone steps from the crowd. It would be totally unrealistic.' Even so, additional bodyguard protection was provided soon after the incident.

Nevertheless, bodyguards responsible for the Royal Family's protection will always be fighting both the assassin and the media, especially when the future King of England tells a Spanish journalist, in a rather nonchalant way: 'If your name is on the bullet, there is nothing you can do about it.' He may be right, but a member of his security team added, in private: 'Not if we have anything to do with it.'

7

Human Shields

What makes a perfectly sane, articulate and rational person stand in the path of a bullet intended to kill someone else? Could it be their training, or a sense of duty to their country? Maybe it is the friendship that develops between the two people during years of working together. Or is it all three rolled into one? Some commentators have tried to simplify the bodyguard's motive for wanting to die as a sense of patriotism. However, no one would deny that soldiers from élite special forces regiments are some of the most patriotic people in the world, and arguably make the best bodyguards, though they are not prepared to die in a futile gesture of loyalty.

During my researches into the secretive world of top-level bodyguard protection I was given a variety of answers by a range of experienced people. Most of those at the top of the pyramid replied with a shrug of the shoulders, saying 'I really don't know', whereas bodyguards at the bottom of the pyramid, working in the private security industry, replied in somewhat more detail, 'Because it's my job and that's what I am paid to do.' But is this true? Would a person turn himself into a human shield for no more than a pay packet at the end of each month? To answer this, and the other questions posed above, we must first delve into the risks bodyguards face every day.

Big Ben rings out at 4 a.m. to signify the dawning of a new day. Up the street, beneath 10 Downing Street, a group of twelve suited personal protection officers linger in the dim light and smoky atmosphere of the whitewashed briefing room. Some sit at tables, chatting about the previous day's events, while others yawn or crack jokes. At the back of the room two detectives painstakingly check the array of weapons that lie spread out on the six-foot foldaway table, including a number of 9mm Glock hand pistols, hefty Remington pump-action shotguns and a multitude of Heckler & Koch MP5 sub-machine pistols, all fitted with miniature torches. Beneath the table a box of smoke grenades and CS gas canisters rest alongside a neat row of bulletproof briefcases. Each weapon was unloaded, cleaned and oiled the previous evening. The MP5S silenced sub-machine pistol now comes in for particular attention, being disassembled and then reassembled before being carefully packed into a specially padded briefcase, with a smoke grenade and CS gas canister in adjacent pouches. These last-minute preparations are a daily ritual for the Prime Minister's protection team, and few in the room take much notice.

The team leader arrives and begins the day's briefing with a rundown of the Prime Minister's engagements. It is two days before the parliamentary recess, and the PM has a busy schedule. The day will begin at 8 a.m. with a formal breakfast at Number 11 with the Chancellor of the Exchequer, followed by private meetings at Number 10 with the Secretary of State, Minister of State for the Armed Forces and the Chief Whip of the House of Commons. At 11 a.m. the PM will travel by motorcade to Buckingham Palace for his formal weekly meeting with the Queen, followed at noon by lunch at the US ambassador's residence off Park Lane, London. The afternoon will start with an arranged visit to a hospice in East Surrey, returning by 3.15 p.m. for Prime Minister's questions in the House of Commons, followed by a meeting at Westminster with the Assistant Government Whips. The day will end with a helicopter flight to his official home at Chequers.

Two days earlier, at the weekly briefing, the team leader had gone over the same schedule and assigned tasks to the detectives. Each man has a vital role to play; half will act as the PM's personal bodyguard, normally the same men, while the other half will conduct advance reconnaissance and act as the liaison between the PM's protection team and the local police. In Westminster this poses few problems, as both agencies work closely together, and many of the bodyguards have worked on secondment to the local force anyway, allowing each side a greater understanding of the other's security requirements. Outside London, difficulties have been encountered, especially regarding resources and who should supply additional manpower. A bodyguard with a diplomatic attitude on the ground often comes in handy. The need for a liaison also has security implications, as it is vital that the

PM's protection team is kept up to date on possible security risks at future locations. This also works the other way, the liaison team knowing when the PM will arrive and if he will be late.

After the team leader has given his outlined summary of events a task sheet is explained, detailing all the detectives' duties for that day. Following this, the leader of the Security Advance Party (SAP) gives a detailed brief on all locations to be visited. He has already conducted a fact-finding mission the previous day, in addition to his visits some weeks earlier. This is normally to check routes, including stopping points such as traffic lights (known as red areas); hot spots, where the PM will exit his limousine, areas overlooked by tall buildings, and bottlenecks; areas where the flow of traffic or pedestrians narrows down into single file. The SAP leader gives each area a colour code to identify the possibility for danger: red, amber, blue, green and black.

All vehicle exit areas, stop points and walkabout routes are known as 'red' areas. Here bodyguards will either be on foot or, if mobile, use their vehicle to shield the PM's car. This is the highest state of alert, and protection officers will be at their most vigilant. 'Amber' areas are those where travel is by road, air or water, and bodyguards will change their procedures for each threat. 'Blue' and 'green' areas are inside 'hostile' buildings, normally when the PM is visiting a location over which the protection team has no long-term control. 'Black' areas are the safest, and are usually inside secure buildings like 10 Downing Street, the Cabinet Office (accessible from Number 10), Buckingham Palace and the House of Commons.

The SAP team leader will also state if any outside agency has been requested to help, such as the Special Escort Group, Engineer Search Team, Army Explosive Search Team including dogs, or police counter-sniper teams. If these units are to be used, they must be requested weeks in advance, mainly because they have to cordon off the area and search it meticulously for any devices. Their presence will normally be continuous throughout the PM's visit and for some time after. There are a multitude of other specialised agencies the PM's bodyguards can call upon for specific duties, including military special forces, intelligence agencies and government 'debugging' units.

The SAP commander is followed by the Personal Escort Security Group Leader. After his briefing comes an 'open discussion period', when everyone can probe any weaknesses or request additional details on the protection screen. None of the team is exempt from criticism, regardless of rank, and a newly assigned detective can, and has, taken apart what seems on the surface to be an impenetrable protection screen. In the words of the team leader: 'If anyone of the team takes the criticism personally or resents it, he certainly won't last long here. We run a tight ship. If there is a leak [in the security sense] which someone has overlooked, and that is spotted by another member, it's imperative he speaks up, even if it turns out to be wrong. There is no mockery or slander from the other guys. We don't work like that. At the end of the day we are all professionals and must work as one body of men.' Then he added, with a wry smile: 'But we don't suffer fools gladly either.'

After the formal briefing and a question-and-answer session, the room is filled with idle chitchat and relaxed laughter as the group splits into three teams of four: the Prime Minister's personal protection team, the SAP and the counter-assault team. The weapons pertaining to each group are issued and signed for, later to be fitted inside special compartments inside the back-up vehicles.

The digital clock on the wall clicks to 5.30 a.m. and the team leader interrupts the noise: 'Let's get breakfast and then get to it.' The group files from the room and a few minutes later all is quiet. The only sound comes from the coffee percolator halfway down the hall as it spits out its muddy brew, and the air conditioning as it kicks into life. This is also a luxury fitted in the back-up vehicles, and something the bodyguards will certainly need. Another hot sticky day has been forecast.

Personal protection officers rarely spend any time relaxing during their long and stressful day. Whether the VIP is conducting a meeting inside a secure building or in an aeroplane 30,000ft above the ground, there is always the allocation of resources or the booking of external agencies to be arranged. Presidents and prime ministers are busy people, constantly on the move, and it is the bodyguards' responsibility to ensure the movement is as smooth and safe as possible.

The Prime Minister is briefed daily by his private secretary about modes of transport, and any problem areas he may encounter that day. For instance, if his personal protection officer is not going to be in attendance during meetings he will need to know where he can be found. This will only occur inside 'black' areas. As a general rule the VIP's personal protection officer should always be within arm's reach, but the majority of bodyguards know this is unpractical – though the US Secret Service refused to work any other way until Bill Clinton was elected.

It is not within the scope of this book to go into detail about tactics or bodyguard positions during motorcades or walkabouts. Suffice it to say that there are elaborate Standard Operational Procedures (SOPs) in place that each protection officer working at the highest level must learn backwards. Contrary to some journalistic comments, every trip made by a VIP is treated differently by his bodyguards, even if the same journey is made ten times in a week, as in the case of Britain's Prime Minister, who is obliged to attend the House of Commons for Prime Minister's questions twice a week. As a safeguard his protection team changes the route or method of travel every time. Sometimes he may not even leave Downing Street by the public entrance, but may travel by another route.

Government bodyguards are kept on their toes throughout the day. Not only do they have to stay mentally ahead of the schedule, but they must be in physical control of their current duties. They must also stay in constant contact with the SAP by mobile 'phone, with the counter-assault team by two-way radio, and with fellow protection officers by digital communications. Bodyguards at the highest level are rarely seen to converse with each other when in the company of the 'protectee'. There are two reasons. Firstly, speaking may confuse or hamper their protective duties, because bodyguards are not only looking for trouble, but listening for it too. The first sign of an impending attack is normally the crack of a pistol being fired. Secondly, and more significantly, bodyguards practise the SOPs time and time again, to the point where it becomes almost second nature, so when actually doing the job instructions are rarely needed. Even when 'guiding' the VIP, a gesture with the hand can be sufficient.

Few VIPs seek the opportunity to join that selected élite who have survived assassination, and many go out of their way to ensure that the Grim Reaper does not call prematurely. John Major is now one of those who has joined Margaret Thatcher, George Bush and Ronald Reagan in holding off the gravediggers for a little while longer at least. The mortar bomb attack on Downing Street in 1991 might have been a lucky shot in the dark for the IRA, but for the Prime Minister's security team it was too close for comfort. One bodyguard present at the time recalled: 'It was believed that if an attack came it would be when the PM was travelling the country on the election campaign ... We had insisted on, and got, approval for a variety of countermeasures that were being set up outside London when the attack came.' He added: 'It was never thought such an attack would be targeted at Downing Street ... there were no contingency plans in place for such an event, and it came as a complete shock'. Just as the Brighton bombing had shocked Downing Street into action over its security, the mortar bomb attack had the same effect, and during the summer recess parliamentary buildings were reinforced to withstand a direct bomb blast. Anti-bomb-blast windows were double insulated and extra close-circuit television cameras were fitted to scan key roads leading to and from the PM's residence. Extra measures were also implemented behind the perimeter gates leading to Number 10, which included a bomb disposal officer from the military dressed in blue coveralls being allocated to search vehicles entering the area, and hydraulic steel barriers submerged into the road to stop unauthorised vehicles from passing the outer security cordon.

Attack from the air has not been overlooked either. In the last twelve months, prompted by the incident at the White House in September 1994, when a light aeroplane was deliberately crashed into the South Wall, questions were asked on both sides of the Atlantic regarding the possible effect had the aeroplane been packed with explosives, and why it was apparently undetected by air traffic controllers. White

127

House advisers had identified the threat some years earlier, and in an attempt to counter it the Secret Service fitted heavy machine-gun ports to the roof. However, on the day of the attack the gun emplacements were unmanned, as they had been for some time. It was the old story of having the best defences in the world but not using them.

International intelligence specialists from the British SAS advised that it would be unpractical and unworkable to fit similar ports to the roof of the Old Admiralty Building, which had the nearest flat roof to Downing Street, firstly because they would have to be manned 24 hours of the day by trained firearms experts, of which the police did not have enough. Secondly, if they were to open fire on a low-flying aircraft heading towards Downing Street, they could inflict more casualties with stray bullets, particularly to civilians, than if the aeroplane was allowed to continue and crash. Downing Street agreed, and chose the alternative option of closing the airspace within a one-mile circle of Number 10 and ordering air traffic controllers to inform Scotland Yard immediately if a plane seemed likely to breach the cordon. They in turn would arrange the evacuation of Number 10.

It may appear to many that the Prime Minister is better protected than the country's monarch, and some experts would agree, backing up their case with the fact that Margaret Thatcher, possibly with visions of grandeur, implemented security measures that went far beyond the general requirements of a Member of Parliament, even if she was the Prime Minister. But, unlike the Royal Family, who publish in advance their daily visits, meetings and official engagements, Prime Ministers keep their movements an official secret.

'Your car is ready for your 11 o'clock appointment, Prime Minister.' His Private Secretary, a distinguished grey-haired gentleman with over 30 years' experience in the Civil Service, has never been late in reminding the PM of his official diary. The PM stands from his red leather chair and hands his file-filled briefcase to a waiting Downing Street aide. In the hallway the PM's personal bodyguard greets his boss with a courteous smile and a 'Good morning, sir,' before taking over responsibility for his safety. He leads him to his waiting motorcade, and once his charge is safely seated he moves into the front left seat, saying 'Let's go' to the government car chauffeur. The motorcade of three armoured limousines pulls away and is joined by a cavalcade of motorcycle outriders from the Special Escort Group.

The lead car of the motorcade contains one bodyguard and two Downing Street aides. The second is the PM's car, and the third holds two more bodyguards and an array of sophisticated jamming equipment and radio transmitters and receivers, plus an arsenal of weapons. In the back of the second car the PM is accompanied by his Private Secretary, who begins to brief the PM on the day's political correspondence and other government business. In the front, his detective dials the SAP team leader's car 'phone and confirms that all ahead is clear and 'free' of trouble. In his earpiece he can hear his second-in-command giving the approaching colour zone and, as they turn left from Downing Street into Whitehall, tourists begin waving. The PM smiles and waves back. In the front his detective replaces the receiver and speaks quietly into his two-way radio: 'ETA [estimated time of arrival] two minutes, all clear Black. Out,' indicating to the other two cars, the SAP team leader and Scotland Yard control centre that the motorcade is clear of Downing Street. The radio crackles and falls silent. Minutes later the sound of the PM's secure communications mobile 'phone punctuates the atmosphere. The Private Secretary lifts the receiver and acknowledges the voice of the Deputy Prime Minister before passing it to the PM. Outside in the warm sunshine, tourists watch as the police escort races ahead to stop the traffic on Trafalgar Square, using determined and authoritative hand signals, or, for the more ignorant tourist, a blast of a whistle, something that never fails to get their attention.

'Left Amber, 500 metres,' the team leader hears in his earpiece, and acknowledges the left turn ahead under Admiralty Arch, followed by 500 metres of clear road. The PM's detective squints and lifts his two-way radio as they turn into the Mall, and orders calmly but quietly: 'Mike One, red car 100 left secure, over.' The reply, 'Roger, Mike One out,' is followed by the lead motorcycle racing off to block the path of a red Ford waiting to turn right into the Mall from Horse Guards Road. The possibility that it might be a terrorist blocking car designed to stop the motorcade cannot be ruled out, and the PM's bodyguards are not prepared to take chances. This part of the route is the most dangerous; they are in a choke point with few escape routes, and tension is high. Parked out of view at the entrance to St James's Palace is a green Transit van. Seated inside is the counter-assault team, ready to spring into life and add weight to the personal protection teams' arsenal of firepower. 'ETA one minute, all clear half-amber. Out,' the team leader says into his radio as the PM replaces the mobile receiver and returns to matters of state with his companion. The motorcade's speed rarely drops below 30mph, so as not to present itself as an easy target. (The RPG-7 rocket launcher, a favourite weapon of terrorists, is designed to hit targets moving at slower speeds.)

Ahead of the motorcade, the road outside the Palace has been closed to traffic for some months, making life easier for the escorts, but there still remains a problem with tourists eager to snatch a look at the PM. Police officers on duty at the Palace do their best to clear a path for the approaching vehicles, but there is always one spectator who bangs on the limousine's glass, causing hearts to jump.

Inside the Palace the SAP team leader informs the Queen's aides of the PM's imminent arrival and moves toward his waiting vehicle. Their job done, the team prepares to move to the next location, the US Embassy. Outside in the Palace's front courtyard the motorcade sweeps on to the gravelled surface and the motorcycle escorts peel away to each side and stop. Inside the PM's vehicle his detective puts the radio to his mouth: 'Clear amber now black. SAP one move when ready; CAT two switch to seven in two. Out.' Upon this instruction the SAP team moves on to the next location, while the Counter-Assault Team prepares to change radio frequency to number seven in two minutes (normally after the PM has exited the limousine) to receive new instructions. The PM seems oblivious to the vague and jumbled instructions of his protection team, and continues passing signed documents back to the Private Secretary. The vehicle comes to a stop and his bodyguard steps out and opens the door for his charge. The PM says nothing as he passes into the security of Buckingham Palace.

Outside, the team's second-in-command issues detailed instructions to the counter-assault team via secure telephone in the back-up car's boot. The Prime Minister will be at the Palace long enough to update the Queen on ministerial decisions and ask formally for her permission to adjourn Parliament for the summer recess, a tradition dating back to Victorian times. The PM's bodyguards are given refreshments and are updated by the SAP team by telephone on developments or problems at the embassy. They wait patiently until the 'nod' from a Palace aide indicates that the Prime Minister is on his way, then the motorcade sets off again.

The use of SAP teams is not new. Most of the world's protection agencies have employed advanced reconnaissance teams for over three decades, but only in the last five years has their importance increased within the security spectrum. The teams are responsible for the security arrangements surrounding official visits. They draw up the emergency escape plans, including a list of equipment required for both the personal protection team and the counter-assault unit, and are also responsible for their deployment en route. The SAP teams decide on manpower requirements, and will task external security agencies, sniffer dogs, bomb disposal teams or police underwater search teams to check sewers and the like. Once the area has been checked the SAP seals it, and anyone entering will be security cleared and given a pass, though they will not be able to leave until the VIP is safely out of the area. This idea is based on the principle discussed earlier, that assassins prefer not to die, and so will not detonate a bomb if they are still in the area. If the SAP team disapproves of a venue or route they will veto the trip and an alternative location will be found. To date, no VIP who has overruled his security team and gone to a venue has lived, a fact of which VIPs are frequently reminded, and one which is guaranteed to gain their attention. But for all the advanced preparations, the moment of truth for any protection team comes when an assassination attempt is initiated.

As already stated, the most likely time for an attack is when the VIP is entering or leaving his vehicle. So the SAP team's primary concern is to ensure that the 'debussing' area is as secure as possible, preferably with overhead cover and away from public view. This is not always possible, and when the risk of assassination is considered extremely likely, the option of using a decoy VIP is considered.

The US Secret Service is known to use presidential decoys, and currently they employ Tim Watters on a pay-by-use basis. He is so convincing that the Secret Service are often unable to tell the difference, and on one occasion, when Watters was visiting the White House to meet his powerful likeness, Hillary Clinton mistook him for her husband and waited by his shoulder until a presidential aide politely whispered the truth in her ear. One presidential bodyguard later asked a journalist: 'If she cannot tell the difference, what chance has a terrorist got?', and a common joke inside the mansion whenever the President is seen on public runs is, 'Is it ... or isn't it?'

Personality decoys are not the only ploy used by government security agencies to fool potential assassins. 'Double bluff' venues or motorcades are also common, being especially popular with the US Secret Service and Britain's Special Branch. The Americans used the latter tactic after the Panama incident in 1992 to protect the President and his wife. The world watched as the presidential motorcade, complete with White House staff cars, limousines, Secret Service back-up cars and police motorcycle outriders disappeared from the area in a blaze of wailing sirens. Meanwhile, the President and his wife sat calmly chatting in a duplicate limousine in a nearby street, flanked by presidential bodyguards openly carrying government-issue Uzi sub-machine guns and powerful pump-action shotguns. If, in the unlikely event, anyone had happened upon the secret location and been stupid enough to attempt an attack, they would have been met by a hail of bullets. In fact no-one except a curious journalist found the location, and he was promptly arrested, manhandled into a waiting Secret Service vehicle and driven away while the President was escorted to a waiting US military helicopter, accompanied by two Apache gunships.

The British used the 'double bluff' tactic during the Queen's visit to France in 1992, when two identical dinner parties were arranged at different venues, complete with guests, food, press and a young girl at each, happily holding a rosette of flowers and smiling with excitement at the prospect of meeting the guest of honour. Although the organisers were fully aware of the plan, others were not, and it is not recorded what they thought when the Queen failed to arrive.

Is the use of such decoys imperative, or is it a sign of paranoia? Some commentators say both, but a senior security adviser at Scotland Yard explained: 'Such methods are used on the very rare occasion when the risk of attack is considered high ... It is not in our interest to inconvenience people, but it's also not our intention to lose a VIP, and so naturally the latter must take precedence over the former.'

Back in the days of open-top limousines or 'bubble-cars' the use of decoys was all but impossible, but nowadays, contrary to the 'rare occasion' policy, it has become an accepted norm for VIPs to arrive at a venue hours in advance of the published times, or to arrive via a hidden entrance at the same time as the decoy. Who is to know if the person stepping from the presidential limousine is the real Bill Clinton or his double? He is only seen for a matter of seconds, and even then spectators and the media are not in a position to scrutinise his appearance. Even with the progress in zoom lens technology there are limits.

What is the underlying reason for such elaborate and elusive security measures? Is it to keep the VIP alive, or to preserve the office he represents? Admittedly, killing a former head of government would not have the same demoralising effect as killing the current holder of office. Returning to the question of why bodyguards are prepared to catch a bullet, can it be because of their loyalty to the office rather than the person? The answer is much simpler than that.

During the research for this book it was found that bodyguards at the highest level answered, 'I don't know' to the question of whether they would die to save their client, whereas those at a much lower level answered without hesitation that they would. However, personal protection officers guarding high-level VIPs are the ones who are employed to step into the line of fire without hesitation, as proved in 1981 during the assassination attempt on Ronald Reagan, when Special Agent Tim McCarthy instinctively ran into the bullet's path, was hit in the abdomen, fell to the ground and remained untreated for fourteen minutes. In the words of one ex-Secret Service bodyguard talking to the *Washington Post* two years later: 'He was expendable, we all were.' Yet Tim McCarthy did not take a bullet because he was expendable, but because of instinct.

Personal protection officers employed at the highest level rarely ponder the question posed at the start of this chapter. If they did, they might not remain in the profession for long. We have already seen that assassination lasts a matter of seconds, and it is the bodyguard's reactions during this time that determine whether or not he becomes a 'human shield' in defence of the protectee. That split-second decision is governed by instinct, not by thought. Just as a child instinctively wants to crawl, a governmental bodyguard instinctively steps into the path of a bullet. There is no time to think, question or weigh up the pros and cons; he just has to act.

Bodyguards at a lower level who say they would die 'without hesitation' have already given the subject some thought, so when it comes to making that split-second decision they will hesitate rather than take the fatal step. It is for this reason that the worlds of political protection and private security are oceans apart. Bodyguards who protect national leaders think on a much deeper and more perceptive level than others within the profession. They see the much larger jigsaw puzzle and know it is they who hold the pieces together. The loss of a head of state would undoubtedly trigger the economic catastrophe discussed earlier, albeit on a much smaller scale, depending who the leader was. Bodyguards step into a bullet's path because they know that if they do not, the puzzle will fall apart. Think for a moment about the effect the assassination of a US President would have on world peace, especially if a subsequent investigation revealed that the instigators were Bosnian Serbs. Would the American people accept such a violation, such a travesty? What would the answer be? War?

It is the bodyguard who prevents this from happening, and he plays a vital role in maintaining world peace. Burdened with such a responsibility, death in the protection of the President is an easy decision to make.

8
The Enemy Within

Security was tight around Teen Murti House. The cordon of tanks and heavily armed Indian commandos blocked every road junction in Delhi. Inside the building, Rajiv Gandhi stood over the mortal remains of his assassinated mother with an empty gaze that would be evident again when her funeral pyre was engulfed in flames. Around him the nation mourned and the world looked on in pity and sorrow. On the other side of the country, in a small, remote village, a similar cremation was taking place, but while millions witnessed the former Prime Minister's final moments, only a handful of mourners stood weeping in the pouring rain as the body of her assassin, Beant Singh, was reduced to ashes.

Only four days before, on 30 October 1984, both Indira and Beant, her personal bodyguard, had sat talking at her home about forthcoming public engagements and the proposed security arrangements for them. Also present was R. K. Dhawan, a much trusted aide of the Prime Minister and a general secretary of the General Congress Party. However, unbeknown to the Prime Minister, Beant planned to assassinate her the following day with the help of another bodyguard, Satwant Singh. It would be claimed by a government commission set up to investigate the assassination that Dhawan was also a part of the conspiracy to kill her, even though no conclusive evidence was ever put forward and Dhawan was later promoted to Rajiv Gandhi's special assistant.

On the day of the assassination the Prime Minister had a break from her normal official routine and was looking forward to her television interview with producer Peter Ustinov. Indira's security was reputed to be among the best in the world. She never received visitors who had not been vetted in advance and physically searched upon arrival, and all of her official visits were shrouded in secrecy and conducted with the tightest of security measures. Her personal bodyguard, Beant Singh, had her full trust and was rarely out of arm's reach when she appeared in public. On that fateful morning, though, he arrived early and waited at the boundary between the Prime Minister's official residence, 1 Safdarjang Road, and her office, 1 Akbar Road. As the frail figure of the Prime Minister approached, dressed in a dazzling saffron-coloured sari, he smiled a greeting. Before she could react he drew his government-issue 0.38 revolver and emptied the chamber into her body at point-blank range. Simultaneously, to her left, Satwant Singh appeared and opened fire with his Sten gun as she collapsed to the floor in a lifeless heap.

As Beant tried desperately to reload his weapon he was shot dead by soldiers from the Indo-Tibetan border police, who, hearing the shots, rushed to the scene from their perimeter security duties. Satwant was also hit and seriously wounded, but lived to face trial and the gallows four years later with another alleged conspirator, Kohar Singh. Indira Gandhi was rushed to the All India Institute of Medical Sciences, but the attempts to save her were in vain. Doctors at the hospital were ordered not to announce her death until her son Rajiv, who was visiting the north-western state of West Bengal, and the President, similarly out of the country in San'a, capital of the Yemen Arab Republic, had been informed. In compliance the news of her killing was not flashed around the world until 2.20 p.m.

The fact that Beant Singh and Satwant Singh were both Sikhs and members of a warrior race from the Punjab state in north-western India raised many an eyebrow in the West, and forced Indian security chiefs to state that the Prime Minister had been warned constantly about the danger she faced with such men filling her protective ranks. But Dhawan, her aide, had reassured the ageing Prime Minister that she had little to fear from the men who would, if necessary, lay down their lives for her. Indira agreed, and refused to remove the Sikh bodyguards from her inner sanctum. The decision caused Western observers to ask not whether she would be assassinated, but when.

This is not to say that Beant Singh was always a potential assassin. His record of loyal service to the Prime Minister's office suggested otherwise. Beant had been employed as a bodyguard in one capacity or another for more than ten years, and had never shown any sign of turning against his principal; in fact he had defended her rigorously in private arguments with other scornful Sikhs. No one could deny that Sikhs had their grievances, and these ultimately lay behind the killing, but Beant had never been affected by such prejudices or a desire to get even. However, it appears that his attitude changed soon after the events surrounding Operation *Blue Star*.

The operation was the brainchild of Indira Gandhi, who, in a desperate attempt to quell the violence caused by Sikh agitation sweeping the Punjab and neighbouring states, ordered the army to enter Sikhism's holiest shrine, the Golden Temple at Amritsar, and arrest Sikh extremist Jarnail Singh Bhindranwale, who had taken refuge within the temple. But the operation was a catastrophe from the start, unprepared troops using unnecessary brute force which resulted in the deaths of hundreds of soldiers and pilgrims, including Bhindranwale. Parts of the sacred temple were damaged beyond repair, but worse, its centrepiece, the Akal Takht, which Sikhs travelled from all corners of the globe to see and pay homage to, was destroyed. The outrage within Sikh communities around the world was unimaginable, and many law-abiding Sikhs refused to allow the matter to rest. Two of those who vowed revenge, and were in a position to carry it out, were Beant and Satwant Singh, who met regularly after the incident and secretly plotted their Prime Minister's downfall. Her assassination now became a foregone conclusion.

Beant masked his anger well and tightened the Prime Minister's personal security, deploying the Indo-Tibetan Border Police to provide an outer cordon around her home. In retrospect, Western security experts could see that Indira's bodyguard, by appointing himself her only personal protection officer and ensuring that officials could not persuade her to remove Sikhs from the protection team, had in effect cocooned the Prime Minister inside a killing zone from which she would be unable to escape.

There is no doubt that Beant was a highly respected man, fully trusted by Indira. In the weeks leading up to her killing, at a time when all Sikhs coming into contact with the leader were carefully vetted, he was able to appoint two additional Sikh bodyguards, Satwant Singh and Kohar Singh, whose responsibility it was to provide protection when he was off duty. This certainly seemed extraordinary to British and American bodyguards at the time, and why Indira's security advisers showed no signs of disapproval at the appointments remains a mystery, especially when Rajiv Gandhi had requested on two occasions that Satwant be removed because of his 'odd behaviour'. The fact that Indira placed so much trust in her personal protection officer was her ultimate downfall. Like so many VIPs before and after, she refused to believe that her bodyguards would turn their weapons against her.

Nor can it be ignored that officials who dared to predict such an event rarely remained employed as confidants. Rajiv was informed of his mother's assassination as he flew back to Delhi. Stunned and shocked by the news, he sat a short distance from his entourage but showed no sign of tears. Deep in his own thoughts, he gazed out into the deep blue sky, and one cannot help wondering whether he was feeling anger, hatred or fear, and whether he was contemplating if, or when, he too would become the victim of assassination.

If the assassins had intended to upset the country's equilibrium, they certainly failed. The announcement that Rajiv would take over his mother's role as Prime Minister saw to that, and even before the thirteen days of official mourning had ended, the nation was returning to normality.

Some things did change, though. Rajiv's protection was overhauled in the light of his mother's demise, and the entire protection team was replaced by soldiers from the Indo-Tibetan Border police. The emphasis quickly changed from low-key to high-profile. Bodyguards openly carried weapons in public, and Rajiv's eight-man protection team was never more than ten feet from his side. Even during overseas visits the Indian Prime Minister was accompanied by a four-man team supplemented by additional bodyguards from the host nations' security forces. Whether he was visiting Washington, London or Paris, his bodyguards were requested to conceal their weapons, a demand first made by the US Secret Service, and one that was immediately refused. For these bodyguards were used to dictating security policy, not being dictated to, and were not prepared to fall in with Western protocol. It was Rajiv, a man more used to hob-nobbing in the world's centres of power, who finally persuaded his protection team to conceal their arsenal of weapons.

Yet no matter how good his security team were they failed to prevent his own murder, which came from a totally unexpected quarter and was almost impossible to defend against. Rajiv rarely conducted public walkabouts like other world leaders, and even during the prime ministerial election campaign in 1989 his 'meeting the people' walkabouts were stage-managed by his security team. So when a fanatical suicide bomber detonated the fuse which blew Rajiv and his bodyguards to bits as he greeted a crowd of supposedly 'vetted' well wishers, the apparently impenetrable defence theory was shattered for ever.

Rajiv's killer has never been positively identified, even though the Tamil Tigers immediately claimed that the suicide bomber was one of their martyrs, which certainly fitted with their policy of killing VIPs, and other suicide assassinations. However, many questions surrounding the brutal killing still remain unanswered, including how the bomber came to be allowed through one of the world's tightest security screens without being searched, and why the Tamil Tigers chose the security-conscious Rajiv rather than other members of his government who had little or no protection. Surely they would have posed easier targets and achieved the same shocking effect.

Even the government's investigation into the assassination, set up by Rajiv's successor, P. V. Narsimha Rao, like the Warren Commission three decades before, raised more questions than it actually answered and has failed to lay the matter to rest. More recently details have emerged pointing the finger of suspicion toward former President Zail Singh, who appointed Rajiv to office but later fell out with the Prime Minister because he had been excluded from affairs of state, most notably the negotiations over the future of the Punjab. Rajiv's widow, Sonia Gandhi, has also tried to push the government into admitting that there was a conspiracy to kill her husband, but Prime Minister Rao informed the widow in a secret communiqué that, if she persisted in her attempts to rock the boat, the skeletons in the Gandhi closet would be revealed, a statement that only added fuel to the fire. If Rajiv was killed by the Tamil Tigers, they could only have achieved such a success with help from within.

Outside India, security advisers to many of the world's leaders desperately tried to reassure their charges that there was little chance they were being stalked by assassins within. All the same, over the succeeding months personal protection officers considered 'too close' to their charges were reassigned to other duties, and new appointees were ordered to keep their distance, in the personal rather than the physical sense.

This may have been paranoia, particularly as national leaders rarely had any direct control over who was appointed to their protection team. For instance, the American presidential or British prime ministerial protection teams are controlled and appointed by senior commanders from the Secret Service and the Special Branch respectively. Team members working for both agencies are changed regularly, and procedures governing their conduct are reviewed and updated at the same time. Even if the VIP were to request that a particular individual remain in the team, he would be advised that for 'national security' or 'personal reasons' it would be best if the officer was transferred to other duties, and rarely will a VIP argue with 'national security'.

Without doubt this does reduce the likelihood of assassination from within, but only insofar as the new bodyguard moving into the inner cordon has been vetted and security cleared. For instance, it is highly unlikely that the Special Branch would appoint a bodyguard who had lived in a Republican area of Belfast to the Prime Minister's personal protection team. This is not to say that the Special Branch believes that all people living in these areas have paramilitary status, but it would raise doubt in the minds of other team members, and could leave the VIP open to unnecessary danger.

The risk from an otherwise loyal bodyguard will never be totally eradicated, and the possibility will always remain that an overworked and highly stressed protection officer could snap and open fire. Personal protection team leaders are fully aware of such risks, and will always put the safety of their VIP before political correctness or niceties, and any team member who behaves even slightly out of character will quickly be removed from duty. Protection teams have measures in place to watch top-level bodyguards both on and off duty. Team leaders have to have bodyguards looking both outwards and inwards, and those with the responsibility of watching their colleagues are in turn watched themselves. It is a safety net that has so far worked to ensure that the VIP receives the best possible protection.

Israel was the first country to spot the potential threat of highly trained bodyguards in eliminating terrorist assassins. For not only were they experts in keeping VIPs alive, they were professionals proficient in killing. Soon after the Munich Olympics massacre in 1972 Israel went on the offensive to track down and assassinate the 'leaders of Israel's terrorist enemies'. However, these assassins were no ordinary killers, but ex-military trained bodyguards from the Sayaret Matkal, who had provided personal protection for General Aharon Yariv, the architect of the 'hit team', and Israeli Prime Minister Yitzhak Rabin. Not only did the Israeli intelligence service, Mossad, provide targets, surveillance, information and transport for the hit teams, but on occasions it also helped act as the judge, jury and executioner.

The state-sponsored assassination crusade began in Rome on 18 October 1972 with the killing of Wael Zwaiter by two unknown gunmen, and ended ten corpses later on 27 July the following year in the Norwegian town of Lillehammer. The end came not because Israel had a sudden rush of compassion, but because the roving hit team had shot dead an Algerian waiter, Ahmed Bouchiki, after mistaking him for Ali Hassan Salameh. Salameh was considered by Mossad to be a main player in PLO affairs and the mastermind behind the Munich massacre, and to say he was high on the hit list would be an understatement. However, the operation was a complete disaster. Five of the hit squad were arrested, four subsequently being imprisoned, and two other members, the shooters, escaped and returned to Tel Aviv. But the incident caused widespread embarrassment for the Israeli government, and the unit was immediately disbanded.

Israel's attempts to exact revenge on terrorist leaders had many secret supporters, especially within some Western governments, but as far as defeating terrorism or even stopping terrorist atrocities in Europe was concerned, they had little effect. On the contrary, the PLO and Black September movements dispatched their own 'hit teams' in a tit-for-tat assassination war that claimed the lives of countless VIPs. But if Israel had publicly appeared to call off its hit team, in private the decision was made to continue the search for Salameh, with the order that when he was found he was to be terminated at the earliest opportunity. Admittedly ex-Israeli bodyguards were not involved in this second phase of operations. The state authorities wanted 'the godfather of terrorism' more than any other single goal, and left the planning in the domain of the Mossad.

The Mossad team closed in on Salameh, but this was never easy, for he was not only Arafat's protégé but also the commander of his personal protection team, Force 17, which entitled him to a heavy blanket of security. However, the American CIA were also trying to track down Salameh; not to kill him, but to recruit him as an agent. Once they had found the elusive figure, and fearing that others would soon do the same, they offered him a bodyguard unit from a US Special Forces team, which he promptly refused. Over the following weeks secret meetings were set up across Europe with Salameh and CIA intermediaries, during one of which the alleged terrorist leader was given a blank cheque and told to fill in his price. He never did, but by now the Mossad had caught up with him, only to be ordered by Tel Aviv to back off. As far as the political masters were concerned Salameh was now under American control. In fact they were wrong; Salameh was under no one's control, and terrorism in both Europe and the Middle East escalated to a point where, in 1978, the Mossad made a direct approach to the CIA and requested to know if Salameh was their agent. If he was, they said, he would live. The question was passed to Salameh by the CIA, in the hope it would sway him into making a positive decision, but it did not. He replied that he was 'working for Palestine and nobody else'. The Mossad now had the all-clear to formulate their assassination plan.

What they were up against was Force 17, a highly trained and motivated protection unit involved in the protection of a number of PLO representatives, both in the Middle East and Europe. However, the unit allowed Salameh to adopt a fatal routine of visiting his pregnant wife at her flat in West Beirut, often during the afternoons, then going to a local gym. The Mossad hit team stalked their prey for more than two months before driving their massive car bomb into place.

During the afternoon of 22 January 1979 Salameh was escorted to his waiting car by two Force 17 bodyguards, supported by two more waiting in a back-up vehicle. As the convoy pulled away from the kerb Salameh's personal protection officer for eight years ordered the driver to turn right, rather than to the left as usual. This was not a strange request in light of the operational procedures for changing routes, and was ignored by his relaxed companions in the back. However, seconds after making the turn a bright flash was followed a split-second later by a massive explosion as a parked Volkswagen on the convoy's left turned into a ball of flame. Salameh's motorcade stood little chance, and as débris continued to fall from the sky the emergency vehicles began to arrive. Before them was a scene of carnage and chaos, with burning bodies, mangled vehicles and shocked eyewitnesses littering the road. Israel had finally got its man. Salameh and his entourage of bodyguards paid the ultimate price of their profession. Although the driver survived the blast he died a few days later from his horrific injuries, but not before telling police of the moments leading up to the fatal explosion.

It was asked whether Salameh's bodyguard was a part of the conspiracy to kill him. If so, was he told that the assassination would be carried out in a different way? If not, then his actions seem odd, particularly as he must surely have known that the blast would kill him too. The answer will never be known, but further weight was lent to the bodyguard conspiracy theory when PLO sources revealed that Salameh's armoured limousine, provided by America after he had refused personal protection, had developed a 'mechanical fault'. His personal protection officer refused to wait for it to be repaired, ordering the spare vehicle, which was not armoured, to be used instead, even though the limousine would have been ready in time to pick up Salameh. Was this yet another case of assassination masterminded by the enemy within?

Israel was not the only country to use state-sponsored assassination or abduction teams. Germany, Spain, Italy and France used them in an attempt to keep the assassins at bay, albeit with rather less success than their Israeli counterparts. Britain publicly condemned such operations, but it is known that the SAS used 'snatch teams' to return wanted terrorists to Northern Ireland from their safe houses in the Republic.

The use of such reactive units, including those initially trained to provide personal protection, as assassination squads was undoubtedly counter-productive in deterring or reducing terrorist murders. Even more worrying was the question that, if professional bodyguards were prepared to act as assassins for the state, what sort of protection would VIPs be getting in the future? Could such men and women be persuaded to assassinate the VIP they were trusted to protect in return for a hefty fee or some other sizeable reward? If so, where did that leave the government ministers who had ordered their use as assassins in the first instance when the bodyguards resumed their normal duties?

Not every bodyguard can be so easily swayed, and statistically nine out of ten protection officers can be considered loyal to their principal. To the vast majority even the suggestion of betrayal is scornfully rejected and highly resented. Gaining access to the world of VIP protection requires years of cumulative training and hands-on experience, and once he is in the business the bodyguard is only too aware that by losing his client he will lose his 'name' and ultimately face rejection. Getting in has not been easy, and he will not be prepared to throw it all away for a few extra dollars.

That is all very well, but history has shown that there are bodyguards and insiders who are prepared to turn against their VIP, and if one member of the VIP's inner cordon is corrupt, then no matter how secure or professional the team is, his security screen will collapse like a stack of cards. The attempted assassination of the Georgian leader and former Soviet Foreign Minister Eduard Shevardnadze in 1995 illustrates this clearly. The attack was not dissimilar to the Salameh killing. A bomb was placed inside a parked van and exploded as Shevardnadze, seated in the last vehicle, drove out of an underground car park in the centre of Tbilisi. The Georgian leader narrowly escaped death in what appeared to be just another VIP assassination attempt. However, an investigation headed by a former KGB officer revealed that the van had been parked inside a 'security safe zone' and was triggered by a high-frequency remote control switch located in a nearby building. Few people had the authority to issue security passes to vehicles entering 'safe zones', and the ex-KGB officer concentrated his investigation on this simple fact. It quickly emerged that the normal high-frequency jamming equipment, employed by Western security agencies, had not been fitted to the motorcade's lead car, even though it had been purchased six months before.

Georgian police immediately released a statement that implicated the paramilitary organisation *Mkhedrioni* (The Horsemen), which had helped Shevardnadze to power three years earlier but which he now wanted to disarm, although the conspiracy lay much deeper. Within days police had arrested two members of the group and two top officials, Temur Khachishuili, a Deputy Security Minister, and Elgudzha Ordzhonikidze, a senior police officer. The former was implicated because he had refused to release the electronic jamming equipment and he was the officer who had ordered the personal protection team to leave the car park via the secondary exit against their wishes, thus taking them into the direct path of the bomb. The latter was identified as having issued the security pass. Both men were in prominent positions within Shevardnadze's security team and had unlimited power when it came to his personal protection.

But if Shevardnadze's bodyguards had had their suspicions about a superior official and reported it, it is highly unlikely that any change would have been made, particularly when it is taken into account that complaints had to go through the chain of command, making it almost impossible to question a senior official without it being blocked. She-vardnadze's bodyguards were all experienced protection officers, having worked within the now defunct KGB's personal protection 'Department A', guarding Communist leaders including Andropov, Chernenko and Gorbachev. The personal protection team was also exonerated in a government report that stated they had taken 'all reasonable precautions' in keeping their principal alive, but were forced into 'a choke point' by 'higher authority' and had no control over subsequent events.

It is this unknowing loss of control that bodyguards fear most. Personal protection teams guarding presidents and prime ministers must always know they are in control of security arrangements. Achieving this is almost impossible in many parts of the world, particularly where different factions control the government. In such countries there will always be separate forces, religious or political, pulling bodyguards in different directions, so the need for protection officers to be neutral is often more important than their experience in close protection, which can be detrimental to the VIP.

At the time of writing there are reports of a guard at Italy's presidential palace being suspended from duty on suspicion of threatening to blow up the nation's President, Oscar Luigi Scalfaro, and his daughter. Such incidents only reinforce the fact that, as the terrorist threat subsides in Europe, bodyguards will still be required to defend against the assassin within. However, in the words of one veteran personal protection officer: 'If a bodyguard has decided to turn against his client, there is precious little the rest of the team can do about it.'

9

Bodyguard or Bouncer

Paul Dallanegra, Alf Weaver, Jim Callaghan, Jerry Judge and Jackie Jackson are names that will not mean a great deal to many. Yet when put next to George Michael, Mick Jagger, Freddie Mercury, Jason Donovan and Madonna they suddenly take on a completely new meaning, for these are the men and women synonymous with protecting the stars. They are the best in the business, and earn in excess of £250 per day.

The world of private protection is no longer filled with heavy-handed thugs. Today celebrity clients look for minders with brains, not brawn. 'Discretion and diplomacy are far better tools in dealing with over-zealous fans, and your principal will like you all the more for it if you use them,' said a former bodyguard of the Beatles and Frank Sinatra.

Until the early 1990s the world of private security was peopled by 'bodyguards' trained by the criminal fraternities or not trained at all. Celebrities hiring personal protection did so knowing the profession's aggressive reputation, often deliberately employing the most pugnacious guardians in an attempt to warn *paparazzi* photographers to stay away. But to the tabloid photo-journalist, venturing into the personal space of a star, even when equipped with zoom lenses, is considered an occupational hazard.

The linkage between the tabloid press, personal protection officer and pop personality is very close indeed. Each relies on the other for work, yet the tabloids hold the ultimate power. In the words of one fallen pop star: 'You are only a celebrity for as long as the press want you to be. As soon as they stop jostling to take your picture, you know you've lost your appeal.' So why do so many celebrities insist on paying bodyguards to fight off the best from Fleet Street? Quite simply to keep the publicity hype going on what would otherwise be a non-event, and ultimately to maintain the 'star' as a media attraction. The days of the 'heavies' are long since gone outside America; they have been replaced by more subtle and tactful 'companions', as they are known by many in the business, but they are no less lethal than their predecessors. These new guardians channel their aggression through their mouths rather than their fists. Whispering menacingly into the ear of the photographer often has the desired effect, and certainly generates less publicity than punching him in the face.

Private bodyguards hardly ever use weapons, not only because of the legal restrictions, but also because many only have a rudimentary understanding of the handling of weapons. However, some ex-special forces personnel in both the USA and Britain admit that it would be foolish not to carry a weapon, especially if the client is deemed in immediate danger, whether this be from the amateur assassin or, more often than not, the Mafia or East End gangsters. But these ex-soldiers are highly trained firearms experts and would not needlessly draw their weapons. However, they are fully aware that it is still unlawful to conceal a weapon, and they know that opening fire and killing in the defence of a client will leave them branded as murderers, not 'bodyguards'. It is a complex jungle in which the untrained can often be fighting a losing battle.

For those employed to protect VIPs who are not considered worthy of police bodyguards, the answer to the problem lies in the development of a good professional working relationship with the authorities. After all, it is the authorities' duty to 'serve and protect' the public at large, which certainly includes those individuals who require private protection. These bodyguards admit that many steps can be taken in conjunction with the police to ensure that the client has a total security package without his bodyguards having to carry firearms. For example, the shrewd and professional private bodyguard would contact the local police and explain the threat to the client, simultaneously arranging for the installation of panic buttons linked to the police station to ensure that the police send an armed response unit.

Leaving the weapons carrying to the police in a hostile situation allows the bodyguard to concentrate on guiding the client to safety. Naturally such arrangements become more complicated as the client steps into public view, when the bodyguard is often the only line of defence. But whereas security companies once relied upon the sheer bulk of numbers to protect, which rarely succeeded anyway, other more elaborate protection techniques are undertaken today to ensure the client's safety at all times.

Closer to the bottom of the scale is the night-club bouncer turned bodyguard. These muscle-bound macho men often have criminal records and have served prison sentences for violent crimes, and their usefulness within the world of close protection is dwindling fast. No longer do egotistical pop stars like Madonna or film legends such as Sylvester Stallone tolerate the arrogant and aggressive behaviour these security teams bring. The old attitude that the bodyguard enhances the prestige of the 'star' is no longer apparent either. On the contrary, the star enhances the bodyguard's prestige, and no longer is it hip to be seen around town surrounded by a score of 'minders' or flanked by flunkeys. During the late 1980s many 'cowboy' companies providing such protection sprang up in both the United Kingdom and Australia, although America already had its 'cowboys', still in operation from the 1960s. Many claimed to offer 'the best security in town' but delivered only bar-room brawlers with no real credentials in personal protection, good for no more than fighting, in which they were only too happy to indulge. Some of these companies are still operating in London and Sydney, and it is unlikely that they will ever disappear, even though their respective governments have tried to weed out the thugs.

In fairness, it must be said that good bodyguards outweigh the bad; today the pop or film star minder is a professional in the true sense of the word. Companies such as Showsec, Music and Arts Security, and Global Perspectives are synonymous with high-quality personal minders, not only trained in first aid, defensive driving and self-defence, but also having expert diplomacy skills.

Mick Jagger, guarded by Jim Callaghan off and on for 25 years, said of his bodyguard: 'Jim is the best minder there is.' He also recommended him to Freddie Mercury, who employed Callaghan right up to his death. But Callaghan, 55 years old, 6ft 2in tall and a strapping 15 stone, shuns such praise, saying: 'I look at them [fans] in such a way that they know not to try anything.' Another top private minder constantly in demand in London is Jerry Judge. At 44 years old he has protected a host of stars including Jason Donovan, who said: 'He's brilliant at keeping people away without offending them.' But Judge, too, refuses to listen to such praise, and as the head of Music and Arts Security in partnership with another bodyguard, Alf Weaver, he says: 'Minding the star is ten per cent of the job. It's just as important to look out for the safety of fans.'

The cost of such protection is not cheap, particularly if the bodyguard is considered the best in the business and has the luxury of being able to pick and choose who to protect. The employer of top-level private security minders can expect to pay in excess of £250 a day, minimum, and in the USA and Australia that figure can be doubled or even trebled. To some the money is immaterial. Pop legend Michael Jackson spends £10,000 a week on personal security, and Police star Sting half that amount. Nowadays, personal protection is far too expensive for the star who simply wants to look important, yet there are those who do, and it certainly siphons off a large proportion of their wealth. In the words of one music manager: 'We recommend to our people not to take on bodyguard protection unless a direct threat has been received. A few do naively believe it's part of the show-business scene, but they usually change their mind when they get the bill.'

In contrast, the lack of personal protection can also be a shock to the casual onlooker. I encountered Hollywood idol Tom Cruise by coincidence, while waiting for a flight to London in the departure lounge at Hanover Airport, Germany. Surprised not to see any bodyguards or aides, I asked: 'Where are all your minders?' With that schoolboy smile that made him famous, he replied: 'The more you have, the more attention you draw.' Was this the same Tom Cruise you read about in the tabloid press, I wondered. No, this was a calm, self-assured man, unfazed by all the press attention; quite surprising bearing in mind that at the time his film *Cocktail* was riding high on both sides of the Atlantic, and the previous night he had been guest of honour at the film's German premiere. It was a tribute to him that he had not employed the services of minders, because he thus drew scant attention from other passengers, and walked through Heathrow Airport without attracting so much as a sideways glance from the crowds.

If this form of self-protection appears tame, it should be compared with the other side of the coin to see which is best. Arnold Schwarzenegger, Hollywood's wealthy heavyweight movie star, employs one of the heaviest of 'heavy' protection screens. Fear, paranoia and diffidence rule the Hollywood legend's life, and rarely will he leave the confines of his home without an eight-man protection team, at least two of which carry firearms. Anybody who attempts to wander too close to 'the great man' on his film sets is manhandled away, and when flying abroad his entourage of minders takes residence in the seats around him in first class. Even the hostesses are not permitted to bring him food or drinks, only his personal bodyguard can do that, and when being escorted through the airport to his waiting motorcade of limousines he is surrounded by a miasma of hostility which focuses the crowd's attention instantly.

In both cases of celebrity protection it is a question of style, a style that is set by the protectee and not the protectors. Both Cruise and Schwarzenegger see themselves as 'stars', but while Tom Cruise hides behind the anonymous face in the crowd, Schwarzenegger does the opposite, preferring to rely on a heavy blanket of security costing five times as much and drawing ten times more attention.

A number of stars of pop, film or television often over-exaggerate the risk to their lives. In the matter of life and limb, the worst a 'star' can expect is a quick grope from frenzied fans, or the forcible removal of a personal item such as a necklace, pendant or cufflink, later to be displayed like a religious artefact in some suburban flatlet. The fact remains that the majority of stars are not stalked by crazed fanatics determined to kill. That is not to say that there are no would-be Mark Chapmans (the man who killed John Lennon), but they are few in number and can often be deterred simply by following normal security measures. However, some entertainers do come into the 'seriously under threat' category. Jodie Foster, Whitney Houston and Kevin Costner (soon after his film *The Bodyguard* was released) were all stalked by lone nuts determined to kill in order to steal their limelight, and if murder is not the order of the day, then sexual assault is. Victoria Principal and Sharon Stone have both been subjected to assaults by obsessed male and female fans in Hollywood.

Hiring bodyguards is one solution to the threat, but it is by no means the only one. The American populace believes that every man has the right to carry and use firearms, and any would-be assassin in that country now steps into the arena knowing that he faces death just as surely as the European terrorist does. Surprisingly, the amateur, unlike the professional, sees his own death as another way to achieve his goal and steal the star's fame. Being killed by the star would certainly do that, even if he was not alive to enjoy it. Few stars are prepared to exercise their right to carry firearms, however, and fewer would be able to pull the trigger if faced by a crazed fan. Such American theatricals are only too happy to leave the responsibility of gun-carrying to a consort of bodyguards, and turn without remorse to the security industry for the answer.

Whether the minder employed as the modern-day gunslinger has the ability to judge correctly the time when a weapon should be drawn is another matter. Outside the professional world of political or diplomatic protection, bodyguards are prone to over-reaction, mainly owing to a combination of lack of experience and misplaced judgement, compounded by a lack of humility to learn from past mistakes. Moreover, the training these bodyguards receive is not on the same scale or as professional as that given in government agencies, except in Britain, where a 'private' security company trains Special Branch bodyguards.

It is true that pop stars and film icons do not face the same threats as world leaders or roaming diplomats, but the threat is there just the same. John Lennon was the first, and last, international celebrity killed by an assassin in public. This is surely due to the increase in bodyguards for hire and the standard which the majority have attained, even if they are not at the same level as their political counterparts.

In an ironic twist, this standard is often achieved with the help and training of ex-special forces personnel who, during their time in the military, would have contributed to improving the standard of political and diplomatic protectors. Surely, if they can turn a policeman into a top-level bodyguard, they can do the same for a civilian? But as one British bodyguard instructor with special forces experience told the author: 'Protection teams working in the private sector require very different skills to that of the Prime Minister's team. For example, it would be unusual for a private bodyguard to carry a weapon, so although he needs to be competent with firearms he does not need to be an expert shot. Police and military bodyguards do.' He continued: 'By the same token, police protection officers need to hold back in drawing their weapons until the last possible moment, and only after the assassin has presented a direct threat by showing a weapon. If no weapon is seen, there is no threat, but for the bodyguard in the private sector it's a case of stopping anyone getting close enough to present a threat, whether they have a weapon or not.'

What the purveyors of protection at all levels have in common is in the belief that a threat, no matter how small, does exist. It is a threat they are employed to counter, whether they are protecting the mega-rich pop star who fears the sex stalker or the groupie, or the globe-trotting business executive who can find himself the target of criminal kidnap or ideological assassination. Today, the business community relies on executive protection almost as much as it does on Wall Street. The entrepreneurs who built the bodyguard industry have achieved more than respectability, and the few who make the grade are virtually indistinguishable from the government or military bodies from which they came. For these companies there are limitless opportunities waiting to be exploited in every corner of the world.

Not all commercial fraternities are as fastidious in their choice of client as perhaps they should be, and consequently the role of close protection is blemished into that of a mercenary service. Middle Eastern rulers, riding high on inflated oil revenues, are now more determined to remove the dissident thorn in their side created by minority anti-government groups, and are happy to employ protection teams first as guardians and then as killers of the potential threat. In the words of one veteran bodyguard turned mercenary: 'Why wait for them to come to you? Better to take the initiative and remove them from the equation, permanently.'

The main employer of bodyguard protection has always been the Arab sheik, renowned for not wholly embracing the philosophy of resolving troubles without bloodshed. As long as there are people paying assassins there will be others paying for reliable professional protection, and the Arab sheik is sure to be at the front of the queue.

For millionaires, pop stars and procurement executives moving around the world in an almost mobile community, the guardian represents more than just simple security. He must be a universal Mr Know-it-all, versed in what lies ahead, whether it be the layout of an airport or railway station or the quickest and safest route to the selected hotel. Such information must have been gained from years of experience, because pre-reconnaissance trips cannot be carried out owing to their cost. Another abiding difference from government protection is that private bodyguards work on an agreed budget, whereas political protectors have unlimited resources. The bodyguard must also ensure that his client is not caught in an embarrassing or compromising position, especially if his client is renowned for his pursuit of something more amusing than mere public socialising.

As terrorism escalated across the West and government protection mushroomed to counter the threat, so did the private protection sector. But, as we have seen, assassination posed only a minimal threat to the bodyguard. Kidnap and ransom, known in the business as simply 'K & R', was a much greater problem, and one that achieved better results. During 1989–94 an estimated $60 million in ransom was paid out, though for obvious reasons no insurance company is prepared to reveal its kidnap payout figures.

Kidnapping for money in the 1980s also had other advantages over assassination. Perpetrators had an 80 per cent chance of escaping capture or death, as opposed to only a 30 per cent chance after committing an assassination, though current statistical figures now put the latter figure at 3 per cent, so great have been the improvements in the standard of bodyguard protection. But there were those who were not content with just kidnapping for money, and added other demands not so easily agreed, including the exchange of imprisoned colleagues. Such hostages were always facing a greater risk of death, and would not see freedom again.

This murdering of hostages on a tit-for-tat, death-for-death basis alarmed governments throughout the 1980s, but because of a governmental policy of refusing to talk to kidnappers, the responsibility for negotiating with terrorists was often taken on by private security enterprises. The most prominent and successful of these was, and still is, the British company Control Risks, which has been involved in many kidnap releases in Latin America and the Middle East. Set up in 1974 by Major David Walker, an SAS squadron commander, Control Risks was not dissimilar to KMS, insofar as both provided bodyguards and both were set up by ex-SAS officers. However, that is where the similarity ends. Control Risks is a subsidiary of London-based Hogg Robinson insurance, whereas KMS was controlled and owned by David Stirling. Furthermore, bodyguards for KMS always carried firearms and had opened fire on more than one occasion, whereas Control Risks rarely went in for gun-carrying, no matter who the client was.

Control Risks was not created in response to the growing problem of assassination, or to be a direct competitor to KMS, but to meet the need created by the escalation in abduction, often used only as a means to obtain money to carry out assassinations. Its parent company saw that the art of abduction would surely grow as time passed, and that such an increase would have a knock-on effect, with many corporations turning to insurance companies for policy protection. Hogg Robinson therefore began to prepare the ground in order to offer the best service and also to reduce the potential for loss by employing the best negotiators.

Such companies tend to operate in a cloud of secrecy, and deny to the press any involvement in such work. The official and lawful policy of many governments is not to give in to kidnap demands, but many private negotiating companies ignore this policy and work alone to resolve the problem, often without informing the authorities that a kidnapping has even occurred, a policy that causes great conjecture within senior police ranks. Private security companies pass the onus of informing the authorities back to the client, arguing that it is not their responsibility to inform the police and stating that they are employed as third parties but would co-operate fully with any investigation. Very few of the victims' relatives do report the crime, firstly to comply with the kidnappers' instructions, and secondly, and more importantly, because they are advised not to by the insurance company, which will pay the ransom, and the negotiating company.

The companies were certainly proved correct, and now by far the biggest players are the insurance underwriters, for they hold the ultimate bargaining chip; whether to pay the ransom or not. Their involvement in the deadly game of kidnapping began as far back as the early 1960s, when it seemed almost a hobby to abduct and hold a prominent businessman purely for monetary gain. Yet the business did not flourish until after the kidnapping of Terry Waite in the Lebanon in the mid-1980s. The year immediately following his abduction saw a 200 per cent increase in the number of anti-kidnap policies taken out by multinational blue-chip companies. Insurance brokers were happy with the new business, but for profit reasons were not prepared to pay every kidnap demand, so naturally there were always going to be winners and losers in the hostage market. But by using the expert knowledge and experience of Control Risks, insurance companies were able to judge accurately which hostages faced death, as opposed to threatened murder, within the first 24 hours.

If the insurance and risk-taking negotiators were somewhat reticent about their activities, what was not secret was the effect abduction and isolation had on the surviving victims. The brutality and stress to which victims were subjected, often not knowing whether an agreement had been reached or, in many cases, whether the insurers were prepared to pay up, caused emotional damage which would remain with them for the rest of their lives.

The science of crisis management and hostage negotiation requires deep psychological discipline, expert diplomacy and, above all, tact. A kidnap adviser working for American company Delta Services told the author: 'Kidnapping is a serious business and the nego-tiator, being a professional, will avoid wasting time or energy in attempting to score points off the opposition. He must first confirm the abductee is still alive, and if so get a firm assurance that no harm will come to them, and lastly the demands or ransom to secure the vic-tim's release must be noted. Only then can the process begin.

'These three points are vital at the first contact. Often the caller will be nervous, apprehensive and prone to make quick or irrational decisions. He must be calmed and assured that all of his demands will be met. As a negotiator, it is important to talk as if you are on their side, making them believe that it is a "them and us" situation. Once that has been established, the game of bluff and double bluff can start.'

He concluded: 'The emotions of the abductee's family must also be taken into account. Sometimes the process of negotiating can last in excess of six months. This can place enormous strain on the family. Their moods will swing from co-operative to extravagant optimism to deep depression. You're the link man. It's a bit like being an electrical conductor, you have to take in all that energy but only feed it back to others in small amounts.'

This technique is often referred to as 'coercive bargaining', but its more accepted name is psychological warfare. The game is one where the negotiator is not a player but an 'adviser', whether that be to the victim's employer or, more likely, direct to the insurance broker via the family. The consultant is working in an environment where he knows little about the victim or his captors, and their motives and tem-perament are equally opaque. In such a situation even the smallest misunderstanding can, and has, proved fatal.

Stalling the process of ransom payment in an attempt to buy time, or even trying to negotiate the fee down to a realistic minimum, can have its drawbacks. Terrorist kidnappers are not known for their patience, especially where the release of fellow terrorists are con-cerned. One Guatemalan gang sent its victim's amputated fingers to his parents in a hot-dog roll, while another ruthless organisation in Asia cut out the tongue of one of its four prisoners. When that failed to gain a response they amputated his arms and legs before decapitating him in the jungle, his body later being found by a special forces team. In this case the subtle and skilful approach of coercive bargaining had failed, but it was a mistake negotiators did not repeat.

The success or failure of kidnap negotiations depends upon the skill and judgement of the negotiator alone. Only he can make the instant decision required to avert disaster and save lives. The moral debate about K & R operations, and the skill of its negotiators, is certain to raise many more eyebrows in the future, because it is sure that K & R negotiations will continue as long as criminals, and terrorists, choose abduction as a career. But the question of whether kidnap insurance is right or wrong is one that will never be answered to everyone's satisfaction. Companies with operations in risk areas such as South America or the Middle East have a duty to ensure that their staff are adequately protected, but they also have a responsibility to their shareholders, and must not allow profits to be filtered into the pockets of kidnappers. One answer is surely to pay for K & R insurance, but this seems to imply that insurance relies on the negotiators after the event, rather than good personal protection before it. Many have also suggested that being insured actually invites kidnap. However, the majority of abductions come about because of a perception that the individual is rich, often created by the media, not because they are insured; only 1 per cent are. It is unlikely that insurance sways a kidnapper's mind. Nevertheless, the FBI estimates that kidnapping for profit occurs at least once a month without police knowledge, a tradition inherited from its Italian citizens as far back as the 1930s. Control Risks and its competitors are likely to be busy for the foreseeable future.

For individuals who have not got the resources of a blue-chip company behind them, Control Risks provides, for a nominal annual fee of approximately £5,800, an up-to-date information service. Through a computer and a modem the user can instantly access 'on-line security data' containing expert and detailed appraisals of security risks in any one of over 90 countries, day or night. The Control Risks' report is secretly compiled by either local correspondents or London based freelance 'scouts' employed by the company to 'recce' the country regularly. The information provided for the businessman is so detailed that it can guide him through the airport and on to the safest form of transport, and can recommend the best hotel. The system can also book a room in any one of the recommended hotels at the press of a button, and can provide the company's current personal protection rates if the traveller decides to use them.

Contrary to some journalists' accounts, Control Risks is not an intelligence service but an information service. It neither receives nor accepts intelligence from any government agency, and totally denies any preferential treatment from British government sources. This point is reiterated by a representative of the company, who says: 'We are not an intelligence service but a risk-assessment service. Control Risks is a commercial organisation which stays very much within the law.'

Society's richest people have learnt to elude the threat of assassination and abduction by becoming invisible when in public. They adopt Tom Cruise's approach to low-profile personal security, dressing in torn jeans and worn sweatshirts and driving secondhand Fords. One man has totally disappeared from view, hiding behind a pseudonym and living in a modest back-street flat, the only sign of his wealth being the gardener tending the roses and herbaceous borders. Here lives Mr Money himself, John Paul Getty II, with a lifestyle resembling that of a middle-class white-collar worker rather than one of the richest men on earth. The effect of revolutionary violence forced Getty to flee Rome soon after his son was released by his kidnappers minus an ear. Getty employs, albeit sporadically, one trusted bodyguard in the form of a retired Scotland Yard detective who now freelances, and he only increases this protection if he is about to travel abroad.

As private bodyguards stepped on to the streets of London and New York, sporting Italian suits and designer shoes, on another part of the planet their military counterparts were standing protectively inside the dusty and dirty surroundings of a South African diamond mine, dressed in sweaty shorts and oily teeshirts. Both had vital roles to play in the protection of the rich and famous, or in protecting the trinkets that only the rich and famous can afford. For many of the bodyguards employed on both tasks, it was no surprise that Western society was filled with envy verging on the need for revenge. For those not prepared to spend their gathered wealth on bodyguard protection, self-defence was the only solution. But if it was acceptable for the wealthy to turn to karate as a way of defending against the threat, it was certainly not expected of middle-class housewives. But turn they did, and not in small numbers, swapping their aerobics classes for sessions of rigorous martial arts study. It soon became evident that the art of survival in today's inner city suburbs was as real for the person in the street as the threat of assassination was for any of the world's VIPs.

The impact of such action was not immediately apparent, but when the Ivor Spencer School for butlers advertised for ex-SAS bodyguard instructors to groom students in the art of close protection, including self-defence, it became obvious that the 'fear factor' was affecting every area of public and private life. For butlers, *savoir faire* was no longer enough to satisfy a potential employer; they also had to be crack shots and martial arts practitioners.

Yet the streets of Britain have not yet suffered the appalling murder statistics that continue to plague America. Lax gun laws compounded by a spiralling black market in automatic weapons has, in the last decade, created a society fearful of everyday life. The chances that Britain will slip down the same road grow daily. The appearance of a deadly and stealthy trade in arms, especially within the crime-riddled back streets of Manchester and Birmingham, plus a youthful generation which arrogantly believes that violence is the answer to poverty and degradation, are the first signs of such a transformation.

Today it is as easy to buy a Kalashnikov rifle or a semi-automatic shotgun as it is to buy groceries from a local supermarket. The local bars have now become the newest arms retailer, and with Sir Cliff Richard providing the background, substantial firearms deals are negotiated over a pint of Guinness. Even the British police now admit they are fighting a losing battle. The West Midlands Chief Constable said: 'What we are witnessing is the massive expansion of the gun trade in this country', and while police officers once despised the thought of carrying firearms, it is now widely accepted that protection outweighs tradition and sidearms should be worn by every bobby on the beat. Armed response units of highly trained firearms experts equipped with the latest weapons appear to be the temporary solution. To some extent, though, it is a compromise until the controversial decision is made, confirming that police officers will be issued with small-arms. But that is unlikely to happen until instances of weapons in the hands of children become *passé*.

One weapon that is more deadly than a firearm yet much more readily available is the automobile. Private security companies have not been slow to realise this, and now offer a range of defensive and offensive driving courses. The skill of turning half a tonne of metal into a killing machine is not difficult to master, but can cost naive civilians £300 or more if they choose the wrong company.

Global Perspectives, one of the most respected of all British close-protection companies, is manned by a small cadre of ex-SAS soldiers who have served together, in and out of uniform, for years. Add to this a computerised list of freelance ex-service personnel who have almost invariably trained with one of Britain's special forces teams, usually the Paras or Royal Marine Commandos, and you have the best practitioners of private protection available. But the world of private security is not regulated by specific legislation, and this means that anyone is free to start a protection agency, irrespective of background, training, mental health or criminal record, and not all are as professional as Global Perspectives. During 1988–94 the number of companies offering close-protection training within the UK tripled, while America saw a fourfold increase.

The problem of bogus or 'cowboy' companies has always been there, but it is more acute in the USA, particularly since the military's manpower reductions in the early 1990s saw a sudden rush of muscle-bound macho men welcomed with open arms by the security industry, something from which it is unlikely to recover for some time. Ultimately it is an uptight public that suffers from such ineffectual protection. Bogus security services advertising ex-special forces personnel for jobs ranging from security guards and bouncers to bodyguards litter the pages of selected international and continental newspapers and magazines. But the client will not necessarily get a true professional for his money; more probably an ex-military cook barely out of nappies in close-protection terms. Yet neither the client nor his family are to know that, certainly not while they are alive, anyway.

Advertising for work is an indication of either a new business or a bogus one, for established commercial enterprises offer bodyguard protection work by recommendation, and in today's climate the best bodyguards can pick and choose their employers far more easily than he can pick them. The days when clients scanned a parade of potentials and quipped 'I'll have that one' disappeared along with the mourning of John Lennon. Successive governments on both sides of the Atlantic have refused so far to invoke proposals to license security companies. It would appear that 'keeping the cowboys out' is not a priority for either government, and is not likely to be in the near future.

An exception to this is Northern Ireland, a province that enforced its own measures in an attempt to weed out the thugs, many of whom had paramilitary roots and ideals, and organisations that used security as a way to collect protection money from under the noses of the army. Until the new legislation was introduced, the bagmen were happy to mock the system. Posing as legitimate security advisers to milk local businesses for everything they thought they could get, all in the name of protection, their only advice was 'Pay up or we'll burn you down'. No one can deny that businesses did receive the protection they paid for, but it was those doing the protecting that the businesses needed to be protected from. To this end the private security industry had come full circle, providing the answer to a problem it also helped promote. Yet after the Emergency Provisions Act of 1987, anyone who offered a private security service was required to apply for an official permit. This had the dramatic effect of reducing by half the number of commercial enterprises operating in the Province.

The number of murders, muggings and violent crimes on the streets of Britain has not yet matched that in the USA, but it can only be a matter of time. For the ex-bouncer with visions of bodyguarding and a liking for dishing out violence there will always be work protecting a back-street night-club manager in London's Soho or New York's Manhattan, and for the bodyguard with experience of government or military protection there are unlimited opportunities awaiting him in the world's best commercial organisations. If private guards, security or body, are necessary in a free society, then at some point in the future they may well be called upon to carry firearms openly, as opposed to the current practice of concealment. When that day arrives it will mark a significant turning point for British society, a point highlighting the public's fear that death waits round every corner. So far, few countries have had to revert to such desperate measures, those affected by war appearing to be the most prone, but the new trend is starting to creep into even the most passive countries.

America and many European countries have openly armed their police for generations, but only now are bodyguards from America, Germany and Italy displaying weapons on certain protective duties, and not just when guarding diplomats. One country is now at the forefront of deploying armed bodyguards, both openly and concealed, and it is a country that has seen an increase in bodyguard protection far surpassing the escalation in America during the 1960s. The end of the Cold War may have eradicated the possibility of a world war, but it had its price. The former Soviet Union is now a state undermined by a group far more deadly than any terrorist organisation, an organisation that uses assassination as its first answer to any sign of rebellion. Premature death is now a routine matter at the hands of the Russian Mafia.

10

War Without Frontiers

'We have no Mafia in the Soviet Union' read a determined statement by Alexander Charkovsky, editor of the Russian newspaper *Literaturnaya Gazeta*. It would prove to be a lie.

As far back as the revolution that brought Stalin to power there have been small renegade operations exploiting the people for financial gain. In Communist society everything was governed by the state, from food to petrol and from clothes to jewellery. The Communist slogan that 'every man is equal' was fine in theory but rarely worked in practice. Put together a poor man and the country's provisions and he is always prone to bribery. The state's hierarchy knew this better than anyone, but considered the problem to be limited to a few provincial towns, and of no real concern.

At this stage some explanation is required about the Mafia. The word 'Mafia' denotes a specific criminal organisation characterised by intimidation, torture and murder for financial gain. The words 'Mob' or 'Syndicate' refer to a much larger conglomerate composed of the Mafia plus thousands of state and party officials. Many associate the word Mafia with the American Cosa Nostra, which originated in Italy, where its growth and power were a culmination of victimisation and financial extraction from its own people, before migrating to other countries, most notably America. The Russian Mafia has no connections with its Italian counterpart, and is a totally separate organisation. In fact they are bitter rivals, and a war is currently raging between these two 'families' on the streets of Moscow, after the former attempted to muscle in on the latter's territory. This is explained in greater detail later.

For decades the Russian Mafia stayed in the shadows but kept their straws firmly in the state's trough, sucking out a reasonable but not noticeable share of the country's spoils. As the 1970s turned into the 1980s and the Russian leadership faltered on the brink of chaos with the deaths of Brezhnev, Andropov and Chernenko, the underworld mobsters took this as their cue to prepare to take control. For years they had slowly corroded away the party members, using bribery and corruption, and replaced them with their own people. However, events took an unexpected turn when a new man with no Mafia connections stepped from the shadows and took control of the Motherland.

Mikhail Gorbachev soon built a powerful National Defence Council around him and began to overhaul the corrupt party. Within the shortest time-frame imaginable the Communist State of the Soviet Union was cascading into oblivion, the Iron Curtain literally disintegrated into dust, and the influx of Western aid began. This financial aid, which has so far amounted to $260 billion, was seen by the Russian mob as the compensation for which they had waited. Before the changes they had survived on a moderate income, but now true wealth awaited. However, much of this new-found wealth could not just be siphoned off; too many newly elected officials, not yet on the take, would notice. The answer lay again in the distribution of food and other goods in the capital. The goods would be transferred from the state to the wholesale buyers controlled by the Mafia, who in turn raised the price and sold them on. The militia syndicates took their slice of the profits and passed the remainder to party bureaucrats and other state officials.

The Eliseyev's foodstore in central Moscow was one place used by the Mafia's top brass to co-ordinate their operation. Here, over whisky and caviar, future operations were discussed and the assassination of competitors was sanctioned. It was also from here that the decision was made to expand their operation into the growing black market, where goods were sold for six to ten times more than their real value. The decision was to have a massive impact on the fortune the Mafia made, but was also the cause of a widespread increase in the use of sanctioned murder. The Mafia had encroached upon a domain controlled by the small-time criminal, an independent who was not prepared to be pushed to one side. While the escalation of killings grew, the West arrived with its own answer, and into the arena stepped a multitude of close-protection agencies. Russia became the newest theatre of operations for the private-sector bodyguard.

British companies such as Bodyguard Training Services, Trans Global Security International and the Close Protection Executive were soon joined by an equal number of successful American enterprises, including Argen International Security Consultants and DLS Protection. The teams' first task was to familiarise themselves with who was killing whom, and why. The quest was not difficult, and the bodyguards were caught in a serious dilemma. Should they stay and provide personal protection for criminal fraternities? The answer was not easy, particularly as no individual had at that time been arrested or charged with any Mafia-related crime. Some left, while others solved the problem by setting up associated companies, with no obvious connections to the parent company, using local manpower to provide the protection.

This was not wrong as long as the bodyguards themselves stayed within the law and did not participate in the selling-on of state-owned provisions. Most obeyed the law, but a small minority did not. These tended to be those with more bar-room bouncer experience than actual bodyguarding. Their unprofessional attitudes damaged the reputation other high-standing companies had worked hard to achieve.

One thing soon became abundantly clear to the new arrivals; no matter what side they took, the threads of the capital's most ruthless Mafia led far from Moscow, to the Transcaucasus and Central Asia and back to the old square in the heart of the famous city. The Russian Mafia's newly acquired wealth, however, was only as valuable as the material it bought. For maximum profit the purchase of the state's gold, or even of the rouble, which had seen a massive slump since the fall of Communism, were non-starters. The answer was found in the rural countryside, locked in dusty farm outbuildings and cottages. Antique furniture, gold, silver and other precious-metal items were purchased at a fraction of their true worth from unsuspecting peasants who were all too eager to grab a wad of money that often represented a year's wages. What the Mafia could not buy it simply stole. Tens of thousands of works of art, sculptures, tapestries and icons, many dating back 400 years, disappeared from churches across the country, and an untold number of diamond, ruby and sapphire rings found their way into underworld hands.

Meanwhile, private security companies were only too happy with the new-found business, and unknowingly but obligingly transported the items to many European countries. With each consignment came one of the faction's trusted personal protection officers, changing duty from bodyguard to transport guard. They were the logical choice, as they were conversant in the language and knew their way around. The Russian Mafia saw few difficulties ahead, or so they thought.

All went according to plan until one night in the spring of 1993, when a consignment of Victorian antique chairs was being delivered to Hamburg for shipment on to New York via Liverpool. The British bodyguard escorting the load takes up the story:

'Things were going great. We had just crossed the old East–West Germany border, driving toward the North–South autobahn that would take us to Hamburg and for me, bed. It had been a long hard slog. But in the back of my mind something was niggling me. For the previous two hours I had noticed one particular car, a blue BMW with Munich plates. Normally this would not have attracted my attention, but it had been accelerating to catch up with us and then dropping back out of sight. Something just didn't add up. I reasoned we were in the shit but wasn't sure why or who they were. I said nothing to the driver, who spoke little English anyway, and just went through all the possibilities in my head.

'It could have been an enemy of the client, or maybe civil police suspicious of our plates, or worse, German Customs and Excise. I feared little of the last two. I knew the load was legit, and all our documentation was in order, but the encumbrance and delay they would have caused would have been a pain. I decided to confirm they were tailing us, and told the driver, in my best Russian, to pull into the next service station. He did, and they followed. We left without stopping. Now I was really pissed, and scared. I sussed they were not police or customs after they failed to stop us after about another ten miles. There was no way back, and there was no way I could just order the driver to do a 360 reverse turn on the autobahn, even if he was capable, which I doubted.'

This ex-military bodyguard was no amateur when it came to protective duties. Not only had he seen service in Africa and Central America, protecting military commanders, but he had also been shot twice in the defence of his country. Like many bodyguards at that vital moment he was alone. There was no one to give the orders and this time his own life depended upon his decisions. Yet soldiering in its truest sense was about to take over.

'I decided that, whatever their reasons for following us, this was going to come to a head, and if so, it was going to be on my terms. I told the driver the situation as calmly as possible, but his shock and fear were self-evident. He began to babble in Russian and I told him to calm down. It's bloody ironic because I was shitting myself. Many years before I had been told by instructors that "fear is the greatest motivator of many", and trust me, it's true ... I checked the mirrors and saw the car was about 50 feet behind us, and slipped my right hand into the cavity of my jacket. Under my left armpit and resting against my side was my Glock handgun. I suddenly felt real fear, fear I cannot describe. Suddenly it was like a robot had taken over, call it military training if you wish. The autobahn was deserted, so I figured now was as good a time as any. I slipped the safety catch off and told the driver to pull on to the hard shoulder. All the time I was running through what I was going to do in my mind. If the car pulled in behind us I would wait until someone approached close enough for me to see a weapon. If it was a go I would open the door and open fire; we would then get the hell out of there. The only problem I foresaw was if two persons got out and approached on both sides. That would mean I could only take out one of them. If so, it would have to be the one on my side, which would put us at a distinct disadvantage because he wasn't the driver.

'We slowed and I watched as the car passed and pulled in front of us. We now had a great advantage because our headlights lit up the vehicle, and if they turned they would not be able to see anything. I released the button catch on my shoulder holster and drew my weapon, at the same time moving my left arm across my body and clicking open the door, putting my right foot against it ready to kick it open just in case. I stared intently at the car, but there was no movement from the two occupants inside. I raised the weapon to just above the dashboard so as to shoot through the windscreen the second I saw a gun.

'At that split second I realised I'd f——ed up; I'd fallen for the oldest trick in the book. There was a crack from my right and the door burst open. Before I had time to react, a pistol was shoved into my throat and an American voice bellowed: "Drop it, asshole, or I'll blow ya f—ing head off." He didn't have to say it twice. I glanced over to the driver and saw he was getting the same treatment. My mind was in turmoil as I tried to work out who they were. CIA, FBI, f— knows, I thought, but one thing was crystal clear; these guys were professionals. As I had been watching the BMW to our front a second car had pulled in without lights to our rear. It was this car that these two henchmen were from. I was cursing myself for being duped. Their blatant act of bad tailing had been a deliberate act to trap us, and I'd fallen right into it. I was really pissed.

'The next few seconds were filled with a mass of threats and abuse from both Americans as I was dragged from the vehicle and thrust against the side of the van. The driver was soon by my side, muttering in Russian something about not killing him. I knew that was not their intention or we would already have been dead. Two figures approached as I heard cars sweep up the autobahn, unaware of our predicament. My weapon was picked up and the van's lights and ignition switched off. What they said to me I cannot repeat, but suffice to say that they were from a New York Mafia crime family and this was a warning to our "paymasters" to stay out of America. The vehicle was set alight and we were given a good kicking.'

In fact the bodyguard is being modest; he suffered a broken arm and leg, six cracked ribs, a collapsed lung and is permanently scarred from his right shoulder to his left hip, the work of a cut-throat razor. The driver's wounds were much worse. Unknown to the British bodyguard, who had worked in central Moscow for two years, his bosses were Russian Mafia and his consignment was destined for an American auction house. The American Cosa Nostra's patience toward the new Russian fraternity had run out.

The exact date of birth of the American Mafia is unknown, but as far back as 1880 there are reports of Italian Americans using extortion to support other businesses. The first official recognition of the problem was reported by a New Orleans grand jury in 1890, who stated: 'The existence of a secret organisation known as the Mafia has been established beyond doubt.' Who would disagree that today it is the largest and most profitable secret organisation in the world? The roots of the American Mafia lie in Sicily, where it is thought (no conclusive evidence exists) it evolved after it helped defeat the feudal landlords and stopped their harsh treatment of the peasantry on the island.

In modern times the Mafia's power and influence has been used against its own people, and it has become the worst oppressor of the peasants, imposing its own tax on agriculture, industry and commerce and securing elections of puppet candidates through the use of blackmail and assassination. Scores of political and union leaders have been killed by Sicilian and American Mafia families. Not unlike today's Russian Mafia, its older American foe moved its operation from Sicily to exploit the rich pickings available in the USA. But the American Mafia did not accumulate its wealth until the 1920s, when it controlled all social life in the big cities and the small rural towns by working its way into every business by the use of force and intimidation. That none, including judges and bodyguards, were safe from the Mafia was proved in 1979, when the Mafia's chief opponent in Italy, Cesare Terranova, was shot dead by two men in broad daylight. They had carried out the killing to show the fate that awaited any who dared oppose them. Since that date an average 1,000 victims a year have been killed by the American Mafia. In the light of such statistics it is no wonder that the Russian Mafia considered its position very carefully before resuming its excursions to America. But resume them it did, with near-fatal consequences.

Not that the American Mafia objected to the selling of goods for much needed cash; on the contrary, most of the auction houses were owned by the Mafia, which took its slice of the profits. It was the underlying fact that the money was used to buy narcotics that were to be sold in America, a domain controlled by La Cosa Nostra and which nets them an estimated $1 billion a year. Selling antiques was one thing, but narcotics was another.

The Russian Mafia was not prepared to be intimidated, and continued the shipments, losing an estimated half of them through the destructive actions of the Mafia in America. As the tension grew throughout 1993-4 the American syndicate made the critical decision to carry out a pre-emptive assassination of a top player in the Russian family. Days later, and on one of Moscow's busiest roads, a shot rang out, followed by another. The shopping populace froze in shock as the two murderers ran to their waiting car and made their escape. The assassination on a busy street in broad daylight bore all the hallmarks of a mob 'hit', but, unknown to Moscow police detectives who investigated the murder at the time, this was no ordinary killing. It was an assassination that had international connections, and it was to change the face of organised international crime for ever. In the eyes of the Russian Mafia the killing was a declaration of war, but it was a war they were not ready to fight, whereas their foe, with over a century of existence and global connections, happily waited for the wolf to come out of its den.

Stuck in the middle of these two syndicates, like somebody about to referee a boxing match, were the Western bodyguards. But wisdom and experience got the better of financial security, and many companies slowly moved their operations toward protecting the government sector. As one team leader put it: 'In a time of criminal infighting it is usually those attempting to bring peace through justice and arrest who end up becoming the victims.' Western bodyguards offered their services and were duly taken on with warm smiles and sincere thanks.

Meanwhile, Russia's Mafia had to look elsewhere for its security, while America's, on the other hand, already had its protection in place, although not just in the form of bodyguards. The Mafia's long history in America had allowed it to infiltrate all levels of the social tree, little in the way of business and commerce being unaffected. Airports, shipping companies and railway stations employed citizens who had connections with organised crime. These contacts allowed the Mafia the luxury of an advance warning if an attack was imminent. Russian hit men arriving in the country to carry out their contracts were often at an immediate disadvantage without even knowing it. The Mafia's tentacles of death and protection reached out very far, and the number of hit men who disappeared soon after landing, no doubt incorporated in the foundations of a new skyscraper or bridge in Manhattan or New Jersey, will never be known. Neither side can admit to such atrocities, this being the secret world of organised crime, but they have occurred and will continue to do so.

In this cut-throat world the only reliable form of protection was that of the 'made man' acting as bodyguard. In Mafia terms 'made man' means a person who has killed a rival to the crime family, often in cold blood. This is not the brave and heroic world portrayed in the *Godfather* movies, for in the back streets of the Bronx or Harlem the realities of the Mafia are far more sinister and deadly. A man can be killed purely for being in the wrong place or talking to the wrong person. The 'made man' does not discriminate between the guilty and innocent. He has a job to do, and will do it without remorse or regret.

Acting as bodyguard is just another duty he performs for his masters. His standard of training is not close to that of government agencies or even the private sector, but it does not have to be. The Mafia rules by fear, and fear alone. Being a Mafia bodyguard is not about keeping the principal 'out of harm's way', it is about killing anyone who gets in harm's way.

Internal Mafia wars are not new, they have raged in the USA for decades. When the Russian Mafia decided to step into the ring it was totally unprepared for the consequences, taking it for granted that it could compete with its counterparts on the same level. It was wrong, and suffered casualties in the process. Russian gangsters were able to dictate if and when a person was killed in their own country, but there was no such freedom in America. The bodyguards protecting American underworld bosses did their jobs with fortitude and beyond reproach. However, many believed in pre-emptive action and persuaded their superiors to take the fight to the enemy. During 1993–4 676 murders were committed in Moscow alone. It is not known what percentage of this total was related to organised crime, but it is sure to have been high. That is not to say that the American Mafia was the only group responsible. Far from it. In Russia, organised crime is a growing industry that the nation's leadership is unable to control. Western influence and business is flooding in by the week, and there are always entrepreneurs who see themselves as the next high-flyers. Wealth and status in Moscow now appear to be the sole domain of organised crime. The trend appears unstoppable, and so too do the killings. There are only a few vacancies in the marketplace for gangsters, and the only way to enter is if someone leaves in a coffin. Staying in that market and becoming profitable depends upon who has the best bodyguards, yet to afford the best requires prolonged exposure in the marketplace. It is a vicious circle from which few will emerge alive.

Guardians from the world over flocked to the capital of murder to offer their services, and they were certainly not short of takers, even if their own understandings of the threats and duties were somewhat naive. Little publicity had been given to the random murder and mob infighting that plagued the city, and what had been published was often sketchy, incomplete and out of date. Would-be bodyguards desperate for experience naturally entered the jungle with a false perception of the dangers. Bodyguarding has always been a dangerous occupation, but when attitudes are affected by images of suited men donning sunglasses and walking with just a hint of a swagger, it may appear that the bodyguard is nothing more than a figure who jetsets the globe on official 'holidays'. In the real world of Moscow, private security is a deadly business to be indulged in only if life is considered nugatory.

This lack of understanding is shown clearly in the following interview, conducted with a bodyguard who had recently returned from service in Moscow. The man, who will be called Joe, is in his late thirties, and is an ex-coal miner with no military experience. After completing two three-day courses in bodyguard training with a private security company based in the north of England, he decided to take his newly acquired skills to Moscow, with some interesting results.

'My training had been intriguing and enjoyable, and my brief taste of firearms was to me exciting. After completing the courses I felt going to Moscow was the next logical step.'

Lighting a cigarette with shaking hands, he continued:

'I'd been given a contact number by the agency, and as soon as I landed I arranged a meeting. It took place in a packed Moscow hotel during a busy lunch hour period. My interviewer was a distinguished looking gentleman in his late fifties and a younger, more battle-weary man who spoke very little. The formalities were quickly done with and the barrage of questions began. Over coffee and biscuits we discussed security and protection techniques and they scrutinised my training certificates received from the UK agency. The following day I received the call to say I would be hired and my salary was agreed with an advance of payment, mainly to cover accommodation and clothing. I couldn't believe my luck, here I was in a foreign country with as much money in my pocket as some people back home earned in a year, and it was only a month's wages!

'The following day I was picked up by a guy called Steve, an ex-Royal Marine who had seen service in Northern Ireland and the Falklands and had been here for about six months. I remember thinking that if he could survive here that long so could I. Being the team leader he laid out what was expected of me and gave a brief history of the client's work, personal life, threats and future engagements. He also said that I was replacing an experienced bodyguard who had been complacent. Stupidly I took this as meaning he had been fired. He actually meant, as I found out later, that he had been killed.

'The following days I remember were spent waiting in hotels and sitting in cars; the client was actually out of the country but we had to pretend he wasn't. One incident that occurred around this time sticks vividly in my mind. While seated in a busy bar one evening with Steve and another bodyguard, an ex-Green Beret, a tower of a man with arms the size of tree trunks who had experienced combat in Grenada, the Gulf and Panama, sipping my gin and tonic as slowly as possible, Steve suddenly asked what weapon I preferred to use. I was taken aback; my training had been swayed towards unarmed combat, and better still, keeping the client away from trouble. I replied that I carried no weapon. My two colleagues exchanged concerned glances and I suddenly felt very uncomfortable. Looking back on it, I should have got out of there right then. However, Steve calmly put a Glock handgun on the bar and politely told me to take it. His message was clear: "Don't be a c—t. Around here the only thing that keeps you alive is that, and you'd better know how to use it." In one movement I collected up the weapon and slipped it into my pocket, followed by a nervous glance around to see if anyone had noticed. Even if they had, I don't think they cared.

'I had come to Moscow, and into the bodyguard profession, to keep people alive, not to kill them. It suddenly dawned on me that in order to do the former I may have to commit the latter. I grew up that night, but not enough.

'Some weeks later my first dice with death occurred. The client had returned, and on doing so had taken Steve to one side. He came back and in no uncertain terms told us to switch on because trouble was ahead. At that point I was not aware that the client's business interests were criminal, and that this made him a marked man.

'The day had gone smoothly enough when we arrived at our last engagement. The two cars pulled up and I stepped out of the back-up vehicle and moved into position at the rear and to the right of the client, in what is known as a four-man 'box formation'. As I did so, I heard a dull thud from my left and turned to see Steve, who was standing front left, hitting the floor. Shock, confusion and panic swept over me and I froze. After what seemed like an hour but was in fact just a few seconds I realised it was a hit. A short burst of automatic gunfire followed as the ex-Green Beret returned fire from his Uzi, and I lifted the client so he was running on his toes and rushed him forward into the safety of the hotel. Stunned faces of staff greeted us as I steered the boss to the nearest elevator. As we entered the lift and travelled to the fourth floor I checked to ensure the boss was not hit, but my real thoughts were on whether Steve was alive.

'The uncertainty continued for some time as sirens wailed outside as police and ambulances converged on the area. The 'phone rang and I answered it with trepidation. I will always remember Steve's voice saying, matter-of-factly: "Is the boss all right?" Relief, excitement and pleasure filled me as I replied in monosyllables. When I told the boss, he was totally unconcerned, he just continued his work.

'Steve was saved that day only by his bulletproof vest, something I did not have, and in fact although I had carried a weapon it was unloaded. I was foolish putting my life on the line in preference for sending my money back to the UK and living on a small allowance. I realised that if it had been me who had been hit at point-blank range by a 9mm bullet I'd be dead, and no one would have given a toss. After this incident my attitude changed totally toward the world of close protection, and all my remaining pay went on personal protection equipment.'

Asked whether he had taken his role too lightly at first, he replied:

'My theory on close protection was excellent. Put me in any scenario and I'd give a textbook answer, no problem, but at the end of the day I'd had no realistic training. All my work had been done on firing ranges or with blank rounds. Don't get me wrong, the private security industry in Britain is filled with highly professional bodyguards, but when it comes to training others they are restricted in the role-playing they can do, which certainly does not help people like me. I cannot deny that I was told to buy the best equipment available; ballistic armour, shoulder holster, weapon, etc. But at the time it went straight over my head.'

This attitude is not uncommon. Many private protection officers from non-military or government backgrounds expressed similar feelings. The realities on the streets of a war-torn city, or one immersed in gangster warfare, are different to those of a controlled firing range. In Moscow and some American back streets death literally waits round every corner. This is not paranoia, it is a fact, and too many bodyguards are thrown into this cauldron with no real expectations of how hot it is going to be.

Our ex-coal miner's employment ended after nine months and seventeen shootings, two of which were fatal. He still works in the industry, and is currently on assignment in Africa, no doubt much more streetwise and certainly better prepared. Others in his Moscow team were not as lucky. Steve was shot in the face but survived, the ex-Green Beret disappeared while on vacation in Germany, and two other bodyguards who joined the team after Joe were killed in the line of duty. Like so many before and after they were nameless faces. So far as is known, their ex-employer continues to ply his trade on the streets of Moscow and Europe.

Another bodyguard, J. D. as he likes to be known, gave a not dissimilar account of work in Russia, but through experienced eyes. J.D. is in his early forties, with twelve years' close-protection experience behind him. Before that he was a sergeant in the British Army's Parachute Regiment and served in the Falklands, winning a Queen's Gallantry Medal for an act of bravery he refuses to discuss.

'Being a bodyguard is a boring, tedious and thankless job. Yet to be successful requires 100 per cent concentration, all the time. It's no good thinking nothing will happen because nothing ever does. The second bodyguards think like that it's time they gave up the profession.'

With a slight smirk, he adds:

'Yes it can be hairy at times, and yes it can be frightening, but any person with an ounce of commonsense will spend his first pay packets wisely. It's no good saving a fortune if you die in the process. The priority is self-survival followed by client survival. I know that goes against all the rules laid down by the industry, but in this game you can't protect anyone if you're dead, while you'll never work again if you lose your client. It's about balancing the two and hoping to get it right.

'Bodyguards that die in this world are normally those who have failed to either switch on or advise their principal. Advice is the best form of defence in this business, and if he ignores you, you ignore him and do it anyway. You can argue the toss later, but at least he's alive to argue.'

Asked whether or not there are areas that require an experienced rather than a novice guardian, he replied without hesitation:

'Russia. It's becoming the new area of operations for professional bodyguards. Once Africa and possibly South America were the hot spots, but not now. Russia is the place to be. Most novices entering that theatre will be out of their depth. You really do need some sort of military background. Being shot and knifed is a daily occurrence over there, and unless you are mentally and physically prepared for it you can get seriously hurt.'

About his two years there, he said:

'I was under no illusion about the dangers of working in Moscow; I knew from friends that the threat was real. Yet I started my time in the capital with a protection team I had worked with in the Middle East. I knew they were professional and experienced in their duties. Not like many new starters who happily join a team with people they know very little about. In my team we all knew our own strengths and weaknesses, which is vital ... The way to pull together a good team is to utilise bodyguards' strengths; some are superb at counter-surveillance, while others, like me, are crack shots. When working in a 'hot spot' like Russia it's important to get the balance right. We did that and we all came home. There are even some protection teams that have been brought together from all over the world and can't even talk to each other because of language difficulties, which is really stupid. Dangerous as well.

'We had many close scares and were shot at on two occasions. But if you stay on your toes there's never a problem. One incident that I remember took place while we were escorting our man to an art auction in Moscow. We decided the easiest and safest method of travel was by train, but as we exited in the usual five-man triangle formation we encountered two men in hostile mood. No weapon was visible and it appeared they merely wanted to express their displeasure at the client being there.

'In that initial contact I asked myself one question, as did the rest of the team, I later found out; how did the two men know we were coming? The client knew better than to shoot off about where he was going, and I trusted every member of the team, but it certainly looked like we had a leak, which would not be unusual, taking into account the amount of money that can be made for good information. We passed the two men and I dropped slightly back from my position to act as a first line of defence. They followed, and I turned toward them and walked backwards with my hand inside my jacket as a deliberate indication I was carrying [a weapon]. They were not deterred. A few moments later a double-tap [two shots] rang out and I half-turned to my left to identify the assailant. I could not, and the two men stopped in their tracks in bewildered shock. The escort party was by now running, and I had to turn back to keep up. As I did I had to dodge the body of a young man in his late 'teens holding a small-calibre pistol. I was slightly confused, but guessed he had pulled the weapon and was shot dead by a team member. Whether the two men were a decoy or innocent bystanders we never found out, and we left the city immediately after reporting the incident to the police.'

This attack highlights the pervading atmosphere of unpredictability that bodyguards face in Russia. What appears on the surface to be a harmless act of verbal aggression can quickly turn into a fatal assassination, the two being separated by a mere split-second of time. It is in such situations that the élite of the private sector are separated from the ordinary by a bullet.

The incident also underlined how the Russian Mafia were becoming more technically proficient, especially when it came to listening to their rivals. As J.D. explained:

'As a team we carried out our own investigation into the attempt. If we did have a leak we needed to remove it immediately. The client was advised and provided a secret contact within a local bank. His usefulness in checking every team member's bank account for unexplained payments answered one question; if there was a leak, it wasn't a bodyguard. That left the client's staff, but they too drew a blank. The answer took some time to surface, but surface it did, through a mistake.

'The boss's fax machine had had a fault for about three months, and security-vetted technicians were called in on many occasions. This raised little concern until the client decided enough was enough and purchased a new one. Naturally all new equipment was tested for the concealment of electronic devices, but unbeknown to the team leader the old machine was left in his office by mistake. Taking it for granted it was the new one, he proceeded with the scan and got a positive. Concealed inside the machine was a highly sophisticated 'wiretap' bug. The mystery was solved. But now we had to de-bug the house, and in the following days we found no less than eight devices in a variety of machines, from a telephone to a plug socket. It would appear that it wasn't only rivals who were listening in, but the Russian Secret Service [formally the KGB] too.'

J.D. concluded:

'Even after the sweeps we knew there must be others we hadn't found. The Secret Service were highly professional and had state resources behind them. So we implemented new SOPs to safeguard against future breaches in security.'

J.D. is back in the UK, working as a bodyguard instructor for a highly respected agency based in Surrey and hoping to pass on his experience to others who wish to become bodyguards. He said of his new job:

'It's difficult to teach someone instinct or experience. All you can hope for is that they listen and absorb everything you say. They have to be a bit like a sponge; soaking up the information and using it in dribbles. If they can do that they should be all right. But no matter who they are or where they've come from I tell them the same thing: "Stay away from the real hot spots until you're experienced enough to handle it." Yes, you do get the odd gobby ex-soldier who thinks he can handle anything, including being shot at, just because he's walked the streets of Belfast. In fact many see the adrenalin addiction as a come-on. Sadly, though, they will end up either dead or unemployed. Body-guarding is not all hype and action, most of it is filled with tedious routine, monotonous travel and solitary confinement, often locked inside a hotel room with nothing more entertaining than the television or a book. Nights on the town, whether abroad or at home, are out of the question because team SOPs forbid it. Yet few coming into the industry see it that way, preferring to believe the image created by films such as Kevin Costner's *The Bodyguard* or Clint Eastwood's *In the Line of Fire*; an image of prestige, travel and respectability. Admittedly there can be elements of all three, but the majority will be employed to protect the reclusive paranoid as opposed to the extrovert millionaire.'

Close protection comes in many forms, of which the bodyguard is only one, albeit one that has seen a massive increase in popularity over the last two decades, especially within the private sector. Countries such as Britain, the USA and Germany have all seen a proliferation in the number of companies offering bodyguard training, with just as high a number of 'Associations' proclaiming official backing. But the advertisements are merely glossy window dressing designed to entice the gullible and impressionable. The world of private security is dominated by a core of highly respected companies which can pick and choose who they have on their books, and ultimately who obtains work. These companies provide the 'best in the business' and can boast members in countries such as South Africa, Morocco, Romania and Russia. Yet the same companies send their 'novices' into the lion's den, knowing the perils that await them and hoping that the two-day course they have provided will be enough to see them through each passing day.

The trend is unlikely to change in the future, and those intending to follow a career in the world of close protection would do well to seek out a company that boasts little. Personal recommendation is the best road to take when preparing for a career that can have deadly consequences. No one would board an aeroplane and entrust his life to somebody who was not a qualified pilot, so why do the same when entering the world of VIP protection?

Bodyguarding is a respectable career requiring experience rather than technical proficiency, though the two do go hand-in-hand to some degree. The fight between assassin and bodyguard is a war without frontiers, particularly in Russia, and the assassination of VIPs is likely to continue for some years to come, creating a market for covert and overt bodyguards.

The collapse of Communism and the Cold War may have brought a hint of peace on earth, but it also gave birth to a culture that requires the professional bodyguard to see it through infancy. Whether Russia's leadership wants such a dog-eat-dog nation remains to be seen. If they do not, the answer may not be simply to remove the bodyguard, for he is now as much a part of the fabric of Russian society as the woman standing in a bread queue.

Epilogue

Interrupted sleep was something to which I had become accustomed since setting out on my trek through the world of close protection, but by now my travels had come to an end and I had moved on to other projects. The book, just like me, was firmly put to bed. But the ringing in my ears continued, and it was useless to try to ignore it. In the darkness I lifted the telephone receiver, but before I could say: 'This had better be good,' a voice said: 'We have to meet.' I recognised it as a close friend from military intelligence. 'Why ...?' I tried to reply, but before I could finish he hit me with the shock statement: 'Yitzhak Rabin has just been assassinated. But it's not that simple.' I heard the facts surrounding the murder on the news as I drove down the M5 motorway through heavy rain to our meeting.

The assassination of a world leader always creates shock waves that unsettle the world, but when that leader happens to be the central figure in the Palestinian peace negotiations it creates an irrepressible earthquake. Even after the mysterious 'phone call, doubt was already seeded within my mind. The Israeli Prime Minister was reputed to have the tightest security screen outside America; a blanket of cover highly respected by many of the world's close-protection agencies, and one that was copied the world over. The nagging question would not leave my mind: 'What went wrong?'

On the night of Sunday 5 November 1995, as the Israeli Prime Minister was entering his armoured limousine, Yigal Amir stepped from the cheering crowd and opened fire from less than two feet, firing three rounds. Two hit Rabin and proved fatal, while the third hit a bodyguard. As the lifeless Rabin was pushed into his limousine by a second bodyguard and it screeched away at high speed to a nearby hospital, Amir was wrestled to the ground and disarmed by a phalanx of covert bodyguards who had followed him from the crowd. Rabin was the first Prime Minister of Israel to be assassinated, and the only one born in the country.

Like so many of his fellow leaders, Rabin had always lived under the threat of death, and supposedly had in place a protection screen that could match any threat. That screen was provided by an unnamed joint military and police unit that came under the operational control of the *Shin Bet*, the once-vaunted Israeli equivalent of MI5 or the CIA. The bodyguards attached to the unit were trained not only by in-house special forces, but also by the US Secret Service. It was known that his close-protection party had been increased some weeks before the assassination. However, on that fateful night he was escorted by only two bodyguards, with no secondary back-up except his covert bodyguards placed in the crowd.

The motive behind Rabin's assassination was not difficult to understand. In 1993 he had signed the historic peace deal in America with the once-terrorist PLO organisation led by Yasser Arafat, agreeing to the return of territory under dispute by the Palestinians, including the controversial West Bank where over 140,000 Jews had settled. As the peace process with the Palestinians advanced, the fanaticism of the Israeli extreme right became more violent towards the government ministers whom it accused of giving back territory regarded as 'Eretz Israel', or the 'biblical land of Israel'. One such shadowy group, the Eyal (a fighting Jewish organisation), stood out from the rest with its repeated threats against Rabin. Eyal was an offshoot of the outlawed anti-Arab Kach movement founded by the late Rabbi Meir Kahane, an American Jew assassinated by an Arab gunman in New York. These groups had made a hero of Barukh Goldstein, the settler from Brooklyn who massacred 30 Palestinian worshippers in a Hebron mosque in 1994. Both groups believed that the only way to stop the process that would lead to an independent Palestinian state was to assassinate Rabin.

In the aftermath of the assassination the Israeli internal security service, *Shin Bet*, imposed an iron curtain of security measures, including the deployment of special forces soldiers acting as bodyguards. A country that was famed for its openness was retreating behind a wall of bodyguards, and senior politicians who requested a relaxation of the new clampdown received 'a polite refusal'.

The tightening was a knee-jerk reaction by the *Shin Bet* in light of the criticism from the world's press. Fears of violence erupting over the future of the occupied West Bank were rife inside the political spectrum, while outside the security police tried in desperation to seek out the full story behind the killing. Yigal Amir had claimed that he 'acted alone and on God's orders' when he killed Rabin, but his police interrogators were unconvinced.

Amir, a 25-year-old Jewish law student, was an unlikely assassin. Coming from the affluent beach-front suburb of Herzliya, north of Tel Aviv, he lived with his mother, a kindergarten teacher, and his father, a biblical calligrapher. Amir was regarded by his neighbours as 'an ordinary boy', but behind that image of normality lay a man determined to leave his mark. The police were fully aware of Amir's connections with right-wing groups, and these were confirmed when they found a work praising Barukh Goldstein. Before his involvement with the Eyal, Amir had spent much of his military career in the élite Golani combat brigade, followed by service as an immigration official for the Jewish Agency in the former Soviet Union. He had also lived amid senior representatives of the Yesha Council, the umbrella organisation for Jewish settlers and the Likud Youth, before committing his crime.

Amir's movements on the day of the killing are still unknown, but during police interviews he stated that Rabin was not his only target, and he had stalked the Prime Minister for three months. Unknown to Amir, the *Shin Bet* already knew this, and had known it for some time. They also knew that Amir had intended to kill the President and Israeli Deputy Prime Minister Shimon Peres on two previous and separate occasions. But when the intelligence was provided by the CIA, who had intercepted a number of telephone conversations between leaders of the Eyal, and confirmed by the British Secret Service, the *Shin Bet* chose to ignore it; they thought that if an attack was made it would come from the Palestinian quarter, not from the Jewish populace.

Amir's two other assassination plans had been foiled not by the Shin Bet, but by luck. On the first occasion he was prevented from shooting Rabin when the Prime Minister failed to arrive at the country's Holocaust memorial in Jerusalem, the Yad Vashem, because of a suicide bus bombing a week earlier. His second attempt failed when he was forcibly ejected from a rally after screaming about Mr Rabin's abandonment of West Bank settlers.

The security failures that led to the successful assassination are illustrated above: the failure to heed prior intelligence warning that an assassination attempt was imminent, and the failure of the bodyguards to use counter-surveillance techniques to spot the stalking assassin. Yet both mistakes were only small factors in the successful assassination. The element that proved to be the deciding factor was the lax bodyguard protection on the night.

Television footage of Rabin walking to his motorcade seconds before his assassination shows a serious gap in his protection. One expert within the security industry pointed out to the author that Rabin's left flank was totally unprotected. Yet during the subsequent reconstruction this fact was omitted, and the bodyguard was in his proper position. It is also claimed in the reconstruction that this same bodyguard opened the limousine door for the Prime Minister, but in the original film coverage the door was already open, having been opened by his wife's personal bodyguard some moments earlier. So if the bodyguard was not in the formation position, and did not open the door, where was he? This was the vital failing that allowed Amir enough space and time to commit his act.

The fact that Amir was a Jew and not a Palestinian had a bearing on events following the murder. If the assassin had been a Palestinian the peace process would surely have collapsed, to be followed by the onset of another period of isolation and war for the Palestinian people. Manipulating a Jew to assassinate a fellow Jew achieved its intended goal, not halting the peace process but slowing it down. It also brought to the surface a question that had been simmering in the Palestinian pot for some time; can we trust a Jew?

Whether Amir really was a lone crusader, or whether he was persuaded by others to carry out his deadly act, will take some time to emerge, but the arrests of members of his family, his friends and Eyal extremists certainly suggest that he was not. Another twist in the plot came soon after the killing, when Rabin's wife told the investigators that a journalist had asked her minutes before her husband was killed if he was wearing a bulletproof vest. 'Why all of a sudden a protective vest?' she replied. The prescient newsman asked if Mrs Rabin was not afraid a lunatic would rush up and shoot her husband. 'Why all of a sudden you talk of protection? What sort of protection?' she asked as she slid into the waiting limousine. The next time she saw her husband he was falling dead into her lap. She was not the first wife to experience such an event. The pressman has so far not come forward, despite repeated pleas by police investigators.

Yitzhak Rabin lost his life in the pursuit of peace. Like so many before him he was to become a martyr for his country, yet he was aware of his own mortality. 'The cemeteries,' he was fond of saying, 'are full of people who thought they were indispensable.' It was a typical Rabin remark.

Across the world people mourned, just as they had 32 years earlier when Kennedy was gunned down. In that time the world of close protection had passed through adolescence into maturity. But the failures continue, and world leaders are still ruthlessly slaughtered on our streets. Maybe things have not changed so much after all.

Bibliography

Beevor, Anthony, *Inside the British Army* (Corgi Books, 1991).

Dewar, Michael, *Weapons and Equipment of Counter Terrorism* (Arms & Armour Press, 1994).

Dilshad, Najmuddin, 'The Kidnapping of Diplomatic Personnel' (a paper presented to the International Police Academy, Washington, D.C., in 1971).

Flemming, Robert, *Scotland Yard* (Penguin, 1991).

Geraghty, Tony, *Who Dares Wins* (Little, Brown & Co, 1992).

—*The Bullet Catchers* (Grafton, 1988).

Gould, Robert, and Waldren, Michael, *London's Armed Police* (Arms & Armour Press, 1986).

Jeffreys, Diarmuid, *The Bureau* (Macmillan, 1994).

Katz, Samuel M., *Guards Without Frontiers: Israel's War Against Terrorism* (Arms & Armour Press, 1990).

Nugent, Nicholas, *Rajiv Gandhi* (BBC Books, 1990).

O'Connor, Richard, *To Be a Soldier* (Airlife, 1995).

Reedy, George, *The Twilight of the Presidency: From Johnson to Reagan* (Praeger, 1987).

Scheim, David E., *Contract on America: The Mafia Murder of Kennedy* (Shapolsky, 1988).

Urban, Mark, *Big Boys' Rules* (Faber & Faber, 1992).

Ure, John, *Diplomatic Bag* (John Murray, 1994).

Williams, Dr Geoffrey, *The Corporate Sector* (University of Perth, 1982).

Index